NET-WORKING

EMBRACING STRATEGIC EVANGELISM

TROY GIBSON

Copyright © 2013 by Troy Gibson

All rights reserved. No part of this publication may be reproduced, stored in a retrieval system, or transmitted, in any form or by any means, without the prior permission in writing of the copyright holder.

ISBN-10: 0615779581

ISBN-13: 978-0615779584

DEDICATION

This book is dedicated to the many people scattered abroad in the world that are hungering and thirsting for salvation, present truth and righteousness. This dedication also extends to the many saints of God across this earth that have found themselves in spiritual stagnancy and religious holding patterns that have prevented them from gaining the requisite equipping, upgrade and impartation that is necessary to launch them into strong evangelistic purpose and excellence. Your cries have been heard and now your deliverance, empowerment and upgrade are at hand to strengthen you for your precious and powerful calling! Now is the time to take back what the devil stole from you in order to take dominion in every area of your life, family, ministry and business. I declare that the curse of complacency and poverty ends in your life right now and I decree that the blessings and prosperity of wisdom, knowledge, wealth, Kingdom identity, purpose and destiny are now firmly established in you and shall greatly abound in your life in Jesus mighty name!

TABLE OF CONTENTS

I.   **INTRODUCTION**

II.   **FORMING THE NET**

A.   **The Purpose Of Evangelism**

    i.   What Is Evangelism?

    ii.   The Ministry Of Reconciliation

    iii. The Purpose Of Evangelism In The World

    iv. Gospel Penetration

    v.   Who Qualifies For Salvation?

    vi. The Ministry Of The Evangelist

    vii. Evangelism's Stereotypes

    viii. A Full Proof Ministry

    ix.   Kingdom Translation

    x.   The Need For Reformation

    xi.   The Fruit Of An Evangelist

    xii.   The Power Of Repentance

    xiii.   Positioning Gospel Repentance

B.   **The Foundations Of Salvation**

    i.   Origins Of Salvation

    ii.   The Dialect Of The Kingdom

    iii.   The Hearing Ear

    iv.   Itching Ears

    v.   Faith Comes By Hearing

C.   **The Way Of Salvation**

    i.   The New Birth

    ii.   1st Century Salvations

    iii.   Profession Vs. Confession

    iv. True Witness Vs. False Witness

D.   The Progression Of Salvation

    i.   The Clarification Of Romans 10:9

    ii. The Progression Of Salvation

    iii. Precept Upon Precept

    iv. Modes Of Salvation

III. WASHING THE NET

A.   Kingdom Washing

    i.   The Residue Of The Old Catch

    ii. Implementing Godly Wisdom

    iii. Forsaking Traditional Methodologies

    iv. Prejudicial Evangelism

    v. Uprooting Proselytization

    vi. Deliverance From The Spirit Of The World

    vii.   Preaching The Right Gospel

IV. **MENDING THE NET**
- A. **Kingdom Mending**
  - i. The Point Of Intersection
  - ii. The Kingdom Call To Purpose
  - iii. The Net Menders
  - iv. Mending By Revelation
  - v. Evangelistic Specialization
  - vi. Marketing Campaigns
  - vii. Marketplace Distribution
  - viii. Mending By Prayer
  - ix. Tongues Of Intercession

V.   **CASTING THE NET**

  A.   **Kingdom Casting**

      i.   Prophetic Evangelism

      ii.   Partnerships Of Purpose

      iii.   Parable Of The Great Banquet

      iv.   Highways And Hedges

      v.   Gospel Convergence

      vi.   Prophetic Pathways

  B.   **Apostolic Evangelism**

      i.   The Great Publisher

      ii.   Cities Set Upon Hills

      iii.   The Momentum Of Apostolic Evangelism

      iv.   1st Century Evangelism

v. Levels Of Expansion

vi. Kingdom Multiplication

vii. Ministry Through Multiplication

viii. Hallmarks Of Citywide Mobilization

ix. Regional Expansion

x. National Expansion

xi. Global Expansion

xii. The Model Of Apostolic Evangelism

VI. THE CONCLUSION OF THE MATTER

INTRODUCTION

Matthew 5:14 "……..*You are the light of the world. A city that is set on a hill cannot be hid………"*

Welcome to the wonderful world of NETWORKING! By selecting and reading this book, you have just enrolled yourself into a powerful course of strategic evangelism that will catapult you into progressive levels of natural and spiritual expansion as you prepare to fulfill your dominion mandate in the earth. You will learn terms such as evangelistic specialization, outward expansion, onward expansion, the point of intersection, gospel convergence and prophetic pathways. You will learn the principles of gospel penetration, Kingdom multiplication and the gateways to salvation. You will also learn the foundations of salvation, the way of salvation and the progression of salvation.

Then you will gain strong wisdom concerning the powerful dynamics of apostolic and prophetic evangelism that present powerful vehicles to forcefully advance the Kingdom of God across the earth.

Evangelism is the ministry and practice of using your nets to haul in a catch. The principles that you learn in this book will be aimed at increasing your level of strategy so that you can be empowered to become a wiser and more productive fisher of men. After reading this book, you will be able to form the net, wash the net, mend the net and cast the net into the entire world through strong embracement and execution of strategic evangelism. This is your time and your season to become properly equipped and throughly furnished to do the powerful work of the evangelist. Your upgrade begins now!

Troy Gibson

FORMING THE NET

THE PURPOSE OF EVANGELISM

What is Evangelism?

Romans 10:15 ….How beautiful are the feet of them that preach the gospel of peace, and bring glad tidings of good things!

Evangelism is the ministry of preaching and publishing the gospel of the Kingdom of God to a lost and dying world for the purpose of reconciling mankind back to God by salvation.

Salvation is the vehicle by which souls *become* reconciled back into fellowship with God by entering into the Kingdom of God. The focus of evangelism is to preach the gospel to these lost souls in order to draw them to Christ so that they can gain salvation through the vehicle of the New Birth experience.

Once a person becomes born again, they have then gained entrance into the glorious Kingdom of God to then start their lives over with a clean slate. They are now free from the condemnation of the sum total of all of their past sins, living joyfully for Jesus Christ. When a person is properly evangelized, they in essence, start their life over again on the right spiritual foundations that were previously removed by Adam and Eve's sin.

Evangelism publishes the gospel through the primary vehicle of preaching. There are also other modes of verbal and non-verbal gospel publication such as: literary publications, newsfeeds, TV and radio broadcasts, articles, Internet websites, Internet blogs, social media and many other media vehicles that are powerful agents and assistants that aid in spreading the gospel of the Kingdom.

The Ministry Of Reconciliation

Another name that is synonymous with evangelism is **reconciliation.**

2 Corinthians 5:18 And all things are of God, **who has reconciled us back to himself by Jesus Christ, and has given to us the ministry of reconciliation;**

2 Corinthians 5:19 To know that **God was in Christ, reconciling the world back to himself, not imputing their trespasses to them; and has committed to us the word of reconciliation**.

The word "reconcile" comes from the Greek word "katallasso" which means "to return to favor with" and "to receive one *into* favor".

Essentially reconciliation is the operation of restoration that *restores* mankind back into fellowship with God.

When we are reconciled back to God through Jesus Christ and the New Birth experience, it means that we have been returned back into right standing and favor with God.

Later on, after we have grown in grace, wisdom, knowledge and maturity in Him through proper discipleship, God will then entrust us with the *ministry* of reconciliation. The ministry of reconciliation is geared towards reconciling mankind back to God through the vehicle of Jesus Christ. Jesus said, "I am the way, the truth and the life: No man comes to the Father, except he come by me" (St. John 14:6). Jesus Christ is the only way that mankind can be reconciled back to God. Salvation cannot be found anywhere else. There is no other name under heaven given among men whereby we must be saved. Jesus Christ reconciled us back to the Father by the blood that He shed on Calvary's cross, thereby creating a powerful door of access for all of mankind to walk through it to obtain salvation.

So then the ministry of reconciliation restores the masses of mankind back to the Father through the Son of God so that humanity can attain right standing, right fellowship and right relationship with the Father.

Our only path to reconciliation comes through the Son of God and our only path to Kingdom son-ship in God comes through the cross of discipleship. We must take up our cross daily, denying the lusts of the flesh to grow in grace so that we can enter into son-ship!

The Purpose of Evangelism In The World

Mark 16:15 <u>Go into all the world</u>, and preach the gospel **to every creature**.

Remember that mankind's area and sphere of dominion is the entire earth. When we look at the word "dominion", it comes from a Hebrew word "radah" which means to "tread down, subjugate, to prevail against and to rule and reign".

The purpose of evangelism in the world is to preach the gospel of the Kingdom to every creature in order to reap a harvest of saved souls into the Kingdom of God and also to transform every "creature" of human, business and governmental culture and society by the Kingdom so that the Church can effectively take dominion in the earth.

This means that every system, sphere and entity of the world should be spiritually subject to the sovereignty of God and the operations of those systems, spheres and entities should be used to bring glory to God. God has mandated that the Church must go into all these systems to transact Kingdom business through the vehicle of evangelism.

Evangelism's area of operation spreads in all directions across the whole earth and its direction of penetration goes deep *into* the world system that currently operates in the entire earth.

The word "into" from Mark 16:15 refers to gospel penetration or *penetrating* the world with the gospel. This means that the gospel must drill deep and then spread Kingdom culture to every sphere, system and structure of the world. From there, the gospel must be *strategically* preached to every creature within these systems for the purpose of taking them out of the kingdom of Satan to translate them into the Kingdom of God. When Kingdom environments and atmospheres are established by prayer, then it makes it easier to preach the gospel to the creature in question.

Now when we look at the word "creature", this obviously refers to human beings, however what has been grossly overlooked is that the word "creature" also refers to the tangible human constructs and man-made entities of the world's system that are currently being controlled by demonic principalities, powers and rulers of darkness that reside in the high places of the second heaven.

From a strategic vantage point, they have the high ground as it relates to the world and as such, govern everything that occurs in the world. These are the same demonic entities that control, regulate and govern the direction of all the systems of the world to ultimately give Satan glory. These agents of Satan gain their power directly from the prince and the power of the air, who is Satan. When a legislative entity is created by a governing body within a particular state, this entity is then said to be a "creature of the state". So then redemption, illumination and enlightenment must occur to those people and people groups who head these man-made entities in order for those "creatures" to be transformed into creatures that are able to reflect the light of Christ and properly model the righteousness of God in the earth.

Let's look at how evangelism travels. As previously mentioned before, evangelism spreads all across the earth and also penetrates *into* the entire world. We must clarify the difference between the earth and the world.

Earth is the planet that we live on, but the world is the entire collection of demonic systems *operating* in the earth that influence and govern man-made systems, structures, governments, business practices, family structures, belief systems, arts and entertainment, idol worship and many other elements of human, business and governmental culture.

The world holds humanity captive in this system of control that molds mindsets, shapes human culture and influences human way of life to be in opposition to the sovereignty of God. In essence, the world promotes much perversion, wickedness and a massive anti-Christ agenda whose intention is to spread unrighteousness all across the earth. When this occurs, human culture, by default, will then render its worship to Satan.

Gospel Penetration

Since the commandment is to go into *all* the world, then that means that the gospel must penetrate the *heart* of the world's systems to spread its publication to every branch within the entire organism.

So then evangelism's mandate is to make its penetration deep into the heart of the entire world system, including all of its components and creatures, and then preach the gospel to those people that are enslaved by this system. In doing this, evangelism seeks to translate those enslaved by the system from the Kingdom of Satan into the Kingdom of God. This is the essence of salvation and a great example of deliverance.

But the problem with a lot of our evangelism today is that we are not making the proper penetration into the world's systems, nor are we reaching the correct depth of penetration before we start casting our nets (preaching the gospel). If an oil miner does not drill deep enough, he cannot discover the oil that is waiting for him beneath the earth. If a cave diver does not dive deep enough, he cannot discover the hidden treasure that is located in the deep parts of the cave just waiting to be found. If a rescue submarine does not dive deep enough, then it cannot find the wreckage of a sunken ship or other artifacts that lay waiting at the bottom of the ocean.

So then the problem with our evangelism lies in us mainly preaching the gospel in shallow, comfortable waters to a group of disinterested people who are only too comfortable with their lives instead of us launching out into the deep parts of the world to preach the gospel to the people who are hungering and thirsting for help and who are also searching for spiritual refuge and a better quality of life. These are the people that are just waiting to be evangelized! When we look at the correct motives for evangelism, they are to preach the gospel to whom God sends you to with the intention of seeking and saving that which is lost (mankind). This is what is needed in order to deliver their souls from a devil's hell.

Evangelism issues public proclamations and announcements to the world of God's general invitation to mankind for salvation and then makes that invitation available to be heard by every human being living on the face of the earth, even those that are under the world's sway and influence. The person must then make a choice on whether to accept this gracious invitation or to reject it.

Who Qualifies for Salvation?

Revelation 14:6 And I saw another angel fly in the midst of heaven, having the everlasting gospel to preach to them that dwell on the earth **to every nation, and kindred, and tongue, and people**.

God has made salvation available to every race, creed, color and nation. Regardless of your nationality, you can be saved! And the beautiful thing about God is that He is not a racist. He is not willing that any should perish, but that all should come to repentance. We must lay aside all of our prejudices concerning the people we want to get saved and don't want to get saved when it comes to evangelism because these prejudices will not only displease God, but it will also affect and limit the potential levels of ingathering of our total harvest. Everyone needs to be saved!

No matter whom you are, who your family is or what background you come from, from the time you exit your mother's womb to the end of your stay on this earth, somewhere along that timeline, you will have to be born again.

And we do a disservice to God and to the rest of humanity when we only want certain people or certain people groups to be saved and the rest discarded. They must all be saved! And we must have a heart and a love for all people if we are ever going to properly model the love of Christ. We can easily sabotage our potential harvest when we incorporate worldly prejudices into our evangelism and outreach. The Word of God says that we are *in* the world, but we are not *of* the world.

This is why we must be completely delivered from the system of the world before we can properly minister *to* the world.

The Ministry of the Evangelist

The ministry of the evangelist needs some tedious exposition here because I feel that there has not been enough exegesis and elaboration on the nature and work of this ministry due to a lack of revelation from the throne of God and a lack of passion for genuine soul-winning. Furthermore, I believe that with the passage of many years, religion and man-made traditions have perverted the institution of this office and ministry, twisted its original meaning and corrupted its core nature to be something that God never intended it to be. So as we look at the office of the evangelist, let us examine what scripture says about it.

Ephesians 4:11 "And he gave some, apostles; and some, prophets; and **some evangelists**; and some, pastors and teachers"

The office of the evangelist is one of the offices of the five-fold ministry. The word "evangelist" comes from the Greek word "euaggelistes" and is interpreted to mean "bringer of good tidings".

Evangelists are God's specific messengers that issue public announcements and royal proclamations that herald the good news of the gospel and the message of salvation to the entire world.

Operating in a royal priesthood (Melchisedec), the evangelist is a royal messenger and an official representative of the kingdom of heaven. Evangelists are ambassadors for Christ and carry the rank of diplomats, who are under official orders from the King of kings to go into the world to announce and publicize heaven's will for all of mankind to be saved. Whenever a government sends a diplomat into a foreign country, it authorizes that diplomat to speak on its behalf as its representative. So then the government of heaven has authorized the evangelist to go into *all* the world, to speak on heaven's behalf as its representative, the message of the gospel armed with grace (charis), power (dunamis) and authority (exousia).

If heaven wants to be represented correctly, it will wisely select evangelists that will rightly represent it. **If the right evangelists are not selected to be sent into the world, then that means heaven will not be represented correctly by these messengers.**

When we pray right, God will then strategically send men and women into the world that have already come to full age and maturity in the gospel. Furthermore, they will preach the gospel with the right motives so that heaven's intentions toward mankind will be properly represented and the fields of the world can be properly harvested through the labor of the evangelist. Evangelists must labor to produce a harvest!

Evangelists primarily move in three realms of Kingdom speech and dialogue:

1. Proclamations

2. Announcements

3. Heralding

Kingdom proclamations are royal public official announcements of God's intentions towards mankind while Kingdom announcements are public statements and formal notices of God's will for mankind. Kingdom heralding means to signal the coming of God's Kingdom advancing in the earth through the preached message. Heralding also ushers that Kingdom into manifestation during evangelistic demonstration.

Each of these three realms of Kingdom speech overlaps each other and evangelists will move seamlessly between these realms depending on the needs and demands of the ministry at the time they are evangelizing. Evangelists move in concert with the will of God and will always proclaim the acceptable year of the Lord in the correct timing of God.

Now let's look at the nature of the evangelist's work and ministry.

Isaiah 61:1 The Spirit of the Lord GOD is upon me; because the LORD has anointed me to preach good tidings to the meek; he has sent me to bind up the brokenhearted, to proclaim liberty to the captives, and the opening of the prison to them that are bound;

Isaiah 61:2 To proclaim the acceptable year of the LORD, and the day of vengeance of our God; **to comfort all that mourn;**

These two scriptures epitomize the work and ministry of the evangelist completely by highlighting seven realms of evangelistic operation:

1. Preach good tidings to the meek (the gospel)

2. Bind up the brokenhearted

3. Proclaim liberty to the captives

4. Open the prison to them that are bound

5. Proclaim salvation publicly in the specific timing of God's approval.

6. Comfort people that live in perpetual states of sorrow, heaviness and depression.

7. Perform godly signs, wonders and miracles to produce belief and faith in Jesus Christ.

The primary work of evangelism is to preach the gospel of the Kingdom in order to save souls. The secondary work of evangelism is to deliver these same souls from various bondages, demonic oppressions and possessions and then heal the wounds caused by these types of demonization.

So here we see that in addition to their primary function of preaching the gospel, their mandate also calls for transitioning into strong realms of healing and deliverance ministry to free the captives that are bound in different, diverse types of bondage to produce great freedom and joy in them. This healing and deliverance ministry ranges from casting demons out of people to healing the wounds of broken hearts.

If the evangelist can only move strongly in preaching the gospel, but can't move just as strongly in healing and deliverance ministry, then they are not thoroughly equipped to fully execute the ministry of the evangelist.

Now let's look at the evangelist's grace, anointing and capacity for heralding and producing harvest.

Luke 10:1 After these things the Lord appointed seventy, <u>and sent them two by two before his face into every city and place, where he himself would come</u>.

Notice that verse one says that the Lord appointed seventy and then sent them into every city and place where He Himself had the intention of going to visit personally. Remember that evangelists operate as heralds. **Heralds are forerunners of God that come into a city, territory or region ahead of God to signal to that territory the oncoming advancement of the Kingdom of God in the specific places that God is getting ready to visit.**

This can be further highlighted by John the Baptist emerging out of the wilderness to preach to Israel that people should repent because the kingdom of heaven was at hand and then later baptizing these repentant souls with the baptism of repentance in the river Jordan (Matthew 3:1-3). John was the forerunner of Christ who heralded the oncoming advancement of Christ's Kingdom. This was later fulfilled when Jesus Christ Himself also emerged from His wilderness testing to preach to Israel that they also should repent because the same kingdom that John preached about was very near to coming into fulfillment (Matthew 4:17). Matthew 4:17 also says, "from that time", which is significant because proper heralding of the Kingdom of God can only come when the time is fully ripe. Wherever God has purposed to visit, He will send His forerunners ahead of Him to announce His arrival. God designates the time and the place that His evangelists must go to herald His coming, which is usually the time right before He gets ready to make a visitation upon that land.

Luke 10:2 <u>Therefore he said to them, The harvest truly is great, but the laborers are few: therefore pray that the Lord of the harvest sends forth laborers into his harvest</u>.

Evangelists sent by God are expert harvesters that harvest the fields of the world to reap the saved souls of mankind at times and places where the harvest is fully ripe. Even as the Father sent the Son of God into the world to be the Savior of mankind, so does the Father send the sons of God into the world walking in the mantle of the evangelist to be strong instruments of harvest, whose expertise lay in harvesting the lost souls of mankind from the system of the world into the Kingdom of God.

The evangelist, as with all offices of the five-fold ministry, is not a gender-specific office and that is why both men and women (that God has called and sent) can execute this office with God's full blessing. The office of the evangelist was birthed from the womb of the Church, whose commencement began at the start of the dispensation of grace in the New Testament. The dispensation of grace (and its demonstrations) began with the institution of the Church in the second chapter of the book of Acts.

So then there is a specific grace that God has placed upon this ministry to enable those that walk in the evangelistic office, and its corresponding grace and demonstrations, to have the supernatural ability to preach the gospel of the Kingdom (with all accompanying signs, wonders and miracles) to individuals, persons, people groups and the world's governing creatures (agencies and institutions) to draw souls to Christ.

Furthermore there is a grace on the office of the evangelist to be able to move in other gifts such as healing and miracles. Remember that grace is not just unmerited favor.

Grace is the supernatural power of God that enables us to perform a task, function, feat and exploit that we couldn't possibly do in our own strength.

So then the grace that is on the life of an evangelist is a "drawing" grace that will draw many lost souls to Christ. When the evangelistic grace is executed correctly, people will not be drawn to the evangelist's fleshly charisma, their intelligence, their education, their vocabulary, their vocal prowess with a microphone, their personality or their local church membership. They will be drawn by the power of Christ to believe in Jesus Christ.

It is the power of Christ that is on the inside of the evangelist that enables the evangelist to function in different realms of healing and deliverance along with signs, wonders and miracles. Furthermore this specific grace enables the evangelist to masterfully preach the gospel so strategically that it expertly positions and publishes the "good news" to the masses, and then provides the only answer for the longing cry of the soul that is hungering and thirsting for a better life.

The ministry of the evangelist and the authority of that office originates from God, however the field (or primary place of assignment) of an evangelist is located in the world, not the church house.

So then a lot of the Church's breakthrough and penetration of the gospel into the world's systems will come from evangelists and strategic evangelism in general.

A lot of times the ministry of the evangelist has been overlooked due to crowd fascination with apostles and prophets. Wonderful prophetic words are coveted after and the life-changing gospel and its corresponding fruit are then put on the backburner at the expense of being entertained by a prophecy. I'm not saying that apostles, prophets and prophecy are not important. On the contrary, these ministries are very important, but the importance of evangelists and their ministries cannot be overlooked or understated just because we may be star-struck by foundational governmental offices (apostles and prophets).

Evangelism's Stereotypes

Sadly over the years, many ordained evangelists as well as many others that have had the call of an evangelist on their lives (but never came to the place of activation or ordination), have not been used properly in the Body of Christ. There are many churches that have type-casted and stereotyped the office of the evangelist for women only (even though men can also be evangelists) since the evangelist is not a governmental office in the Body of Christ. Usually this occurs in churches that don't have strong prophetic ministries and are governed by the spirit of religion, male chauvinism and male dominance.

The spirit of religion is a system of control and error operating in the world that is intended to misinform, misalign and misplace the saints of God out of their God-ordained purpose into a false purpose where they cannot be effective in their specific godly purpose and ministry. Furthermore, the spirit of religion also prevents a person from truly becoming born again and also prevents a person from *growing and progressing* in Christ.

So then women have been automatically and unfairly labeled, stereotyped and type-cast as evangelists because of many senior leaders male chauvinism that continually dominates their entire thought processes on ministry placement. Because of this error, many women have been improperly assigned to work the altar even when they may or may not have the evangelistic call on their lives. Here they do altar work most of the time, helping souls tarry (wait) for the Holy Ghost, taking prayer requests and praying for these requests. Then after that work is done, they are assigned to do other helps ministries, cooking in the kitchen and cleaning the church house while the bishop, pastor and the elders do all the preaching of the gospel. This is an incorrect use of the office of the evangelist and women in evangelism because the primary mission of an evangelist is to preach the gospel to the lost that are located in the world, not the church house.

This has been the cause of a huge spirit of error in this area for many years because many leaders are unwilling to yield to the direction of the Holy Spirit in their choice of ministry selection and furthermore have a warped view on evangelism and outreach.

This is why many evangelists have been frustrated with the spiritual confinement of their local churches because their office and place of assignment was not meant to be confined within the four walls of the church house. Their ministries must go mobile! Additionally, because of the confinement and the general apathy to the call of evangelism, there has not been a huge focus on reaching the lost that are *in the world* whose souls need saving because of many senior leaders contentment with the existing congregational numbers and the corresponding status quo.

The four walls of church have become a prison to true evangelists.

Because of the above mentioned error and little to no passion or strategy when approaching the ministry of evangelism, the role of the evangelist (whether male or female) has been grossly downplayed and diminished to the role of helps ministries simply because their local church and/or denomination has not had the heart or the love to reach out and save a lost and dying world. Because of a lack of agape love and a lack of true evangelistic strategy and direction, the Body of Christ has had a lack of credible, strategic outreach. We have to do better!

A Full Proof Ministry

2 Timothy 4:5 But in all things you must watch, endure afflictions, **do the work of an evangelist, make full proof of your ministry.**

As we examine the work of an evangelist, we encounter the part of scripture that says, "make full proof of your ministry". When the evangelist makes "full proof" of their ministry, in the Greek it means "to carry out fully", "accomplish entirely" and "to fulfill the ministry in every part". This means that no stone is left unturned as we execute this ministry. We must have the revelation, wisdom, knowledge and the strategies of heaven necessary to execute this ministry to its fullness in excellence.

When the evangelist begins to move in their *complete* grace, there will be a clear definition and distinction of what the work of evangelism involves and what is needed to execute it, having already been equipped for it. You will not only see the preaching of the gospel done correctly in power and authority, but you will also see accompanying signs, wonders and miracles begin to manifest and release the glory of God. These miracles could be the healing of people's sicknesses and infirmities and/or it could be delivering them from spiritual bondages, oppressions and desolations. Furthermore, the execution of this ministry will be done in such excellence that it will produce a tremendous harvest of souls ready to move forward in the Kingdom. These souls will receive beauty in exchange for their ashes, the oil of joy in exchange for their mourning and the garments of praise in exchange for their spirits of heaviness. When evangelism is executed to completion in excellence, there will always be a great exchange!

If there is no translation in the spiritual citizenship of the soul in question from the kingdom of Satan to the Kingdom of God (along with its corresponding exchanges), then the work

of the evangelist is not complete and they have not made full proof of their ministry because the souls in question did not experience the great exchange.

Kingdom Translation

Now that you have become acquainted with The Great Exchange, it is now time to become acquainted with the principles of Kingdom Translation.

Colossians 1:12 Giving thanks to the Father, **which has qualified us to be partakers of the inheritance of the saints in light**:

Colossians 1:13 Who has delivered us from the power of darkness, and has translated us into the kingdom of his dear Son:

Colossians 1:14 In whom we have redemption through his blood, even the forgiveness of sins:

Notice that the word "translation" closely correlates with being delivered from the power of darkness. So then there is a strong element of deliverance in evangelism to kill two birds with one stone. Evangelism gets a person saved, but also has the ability to deliver them from the power of darkness. When you are delivered from the power of darkness, then that means your mindset, your conversation, your actions and your lifestyle are no longer being influenced or controlled by the power of darkness or the world system to promote Satan's agendas. The power of darkness no longer has a hold on your life or your soul's destination in eternity.

One of the greatest things about evangelism lies in its ability to multi-task salvation and deliverance simultaneously.

When a person is *translated*, it means "to change the form, nature or condition of" or "to change from a situation or a place".

So then evangelism changes the spiritual orientation of a man or a woman by its powerful grace that has the ability of bridging repentance with redemption.

When the fruits of repentance begin to manifest within a person, then redemption for that person is sure to come next! When men and women are redeemed back to God by the precious blood of Jesus Christ and then begin to move in everything that God says and has promised them, it is in fact a restoration to Garden of Eden authority, godly stewardship and the correct spiritual placement necessary to transact their earthly mandate and responsibility of taking dominion.

Even as Enoch and Elijah were *naturally* translated from the world into heaven, so must we also be *spiritually* translated from the kingdom of Satan into the Kingdom of God while we still live on this earth.

This is needed so that we can legally transact the Kingdom of God in this world in excellence. This is the great spiritual translation that every man and woman must experience in their earthly lifetime. And then once completed, these spiritual translations will inevitably result in the translation of their physical bodies from mortal to immortality and their glorified bodies being translated into heaven at the end of their course on earth when they either "fall asleep in Christ" (physical death) or they are raptured alive into heaven.

The key to seeing if a person has been properly evangelized lies in ascertaining whether they have been properly translated or not.

If the resume of the evangelist does not include a list of people that were *translated* into the Kingdom of God, then that means that the evangelists themselves have not made full proof of their ministries. Consequently, their ministerial credibility as well as their own natural translations into heaven will be called into question when God reveals, exposes and/or judges them. You can't say a person has been converted if they haven't been translated because translation alone is what qualifies you to be a partaker of the inheritance of the saints. So is the ministry of the evangelist producing partakers of the inheritance or is that ministry merely producing spectators of the inheritance?

The Need For Reformation

Once the Body of Christ sees and understands this great need for the translation of the soul and then commits to start moving in this revelation, you will then begin to see the essence of true evangelism manifest all over the globe which will greatly distinguish itself from other fraudulent outreach ministries who only make half-hearted attempts at real evangelism. Additionally, it will also provide a stark contrast and a radical differentiation from apathetic churches who are only concerned with just the "small-time-minimum-required-evangelistic-outreach" church department that only has one or two members who are really admins in rotational helps positions.

Many churches that don't have a love for lost souls do this so that they can spruce up their church websites with a vast array of different and diverse church departments that are intended to show the viewing public their supposed diversity in operations. This is done to make them look bigger and more diversified than what they actually are. This is also what you call smoke and mirrors. With many local churches, their outreach ministries are only an Internet hyperlink on their website, but the reality of the matter is that they don't have fully staffed or full service evangelism teams that are operating weekly in the wisdom of heaven to produce present-day 21st century strategies to reach and save the lost.

But when properly implemented, true evangelism will absolutely revolutionize and lengthen your local church outreach. It will also transform your local church's focus and orientation to send evangelism teams into the world in order to preach the gospel to every creature. **You will know a true evangelist by their anointing, their grace, their work and their harvest!**

I truly believe that most houses (local churches) are not training people to make full proof of their evangelistic ministry. The reasons for this is that they lack the knowledge necessary to unlock strong evangelistic purpose to birth strong training curriculums that will train, equip and release well-prepared and well-equipped evangelists to harvest the fields of the world. Any attempt at evangelistic progress will be severely crippled by a lack of knowledge, wisdom, revelation and strategy which results in ill-prepared ministers that are ill-equipped to undertake such a vast assignment.

Another reason why evangelism cannot excel is because local churches have a lack of passion or caring for that particular ministry because of their acceptance of the majority consensus of clergy and laity with their current state of church membership. In essence, it is a mental and spiritual assimilation into the culture of that church, which has been exposed to the corruptions and pollutions of the world. This culture of apathy has become the cultural norm for every church meeting, conference and convention.

And yet again, it is a lack of proper spiritual impartation by the existing senior leadership that operates in paradigms of ritualistic and redundant ministry patterns that are not geared towards birthing godly purpose. We must first have the correct foundations of local church government, revelatory paradigms of ministry and willing leadership structures that are conducive to releasing the anointing to those that are under their authority. Once leaders have undergone this spiritual revival, they can then impart into their ministers a strong evangelistic grace so that those ministers can then tackle their specific areas of evangelistic ministry effectively.

May I suggest to you that the office and work of the evangelist in the 20th and 21st centuries have not been carried out fully nor has it been accomplished entirely? The reason for this is because of improper teaching regarding an evangelist's function, scope and place of ministry. Furthermore there has been a lack of revelation from the throne of God concerning the evangelist's work, function and grace and that is why, when left up to man to decide for himself on how best to use an evangelist or evangelism in general, most of the time the blueprint was poorly conceived and executed worse.

This lack of revelation can be attributed to a lack of earnest and fervent prayer to receive from God His will concerning this ministry. When we lack revelation, then we will not have the proper instruction necessary to fully equip the evangelist in the *totality* of their call. And if the evangelist is not fully equipped and throughly (completely) furnished for every good work, then they will not be able to minister in their full range of grace, gifting, anointing, function and ministry work in their God-assigned territories. Consequently, they will not see much harvest. Lastly, the office and the work of the evangelist have not been carried out fully because there are yet many souls that still need salvation.

But we must first be competently equipped to be able to effectively cast our nets in order to catch many fish. Sadly, we have not had many training centers, teachers, pamphlets and manuals on strategic evangelism that will properly instruct us in 21st century cutting-edge strategies for evangelistic success to completely furnish the saints to perform every good work.

In essence, we have dropped the ball as well as our responsibility to train our generation on how to reach the lost. If you are called to evangelism, you need to inform the senior leader of your local church.

But if your local church does not want to prepare you for your evangelistic purpose because of extreme indifference to your call or they attempt to distract, control or manipulate you away from your call, then it is time to pray that God begins to connect you with a local church or evangelistic training center that has the passion and personnel to build you for your purpose.

The Fruit Of The Evangelist

When we examine the *harvest* of evangelism, we have to take into account what God actually intended the evangelistic grace to produce.

The fruit of evangelism is first repentance, next the salvation of the soul, and then finally, a changed life.

I feel that we must clarify exactly what repentance is because I see a lot of repentance lacking when people come to the altar to get saved. When we look at the word "repentance", we find that it is a deep sorrow for one's past sins and wrongdoing. Repentance also means that you have changed your mind about your course or path of life that you have previously been walking. The scripture says in 2 Corinthians 7:10 *"For godly sorrow works repentance to salvation not to be repented of...."*

So as evangelism's *true* work begins to go forth, the harvest (fruit) of this work will include a changed heart and a changed mind. When the heart and the mind changes, then that change effectively unlocks the two main shackles (heart and mind) of a person's unbelief.

So then when this dual unlocking occurs, its subsequent openings will break down the former walls and obstructions over the heart and the mind. Then it will open those two main doors of access that the Lord needs in order to gain access and entrance into a person, thereby clearing the way for that person to get saved. Jesus said he is standing at the door knocking and if any will hear His voice and open the door, He will come in and dine with them. The key to entering into divine communion with God is to open the door of your heart and let Him in.

This is why the Word of God says that in the day that you hear His voice, don't harden your heart. If your heart has softened, but your mind still remains rigid and inflexible and vice versa, then you won't ever have lasting change. You may have a temporary change, but not a permanent change. Temporary changes will eventually fall by the wayside and the person will eventually revert back to form with their original mindset and hardness of heart. So in order for a person to have a true lifestyle change, both the heart and the mind must permanently change.

Without having both a changed heart and a changed mind, you don't have true godly repentance.

The gospel of Christ is the power of God, but it will only perform its complete work and will only produce the entire volume of its harvest in those people who will believe it completely and not be ashamed of it!

The second half of 2 Corinthians 7:10 says, *"but the sorrow of the world works death"*. Worldly sorrow is common to many proud and stubborn people. Worldly sorrow means that while it may come to your mind and your heart that you are living a sinful life and are ashamed of your sins and that you need to surrender your life to the will of the Lord, you still refuse to change. A person can refuse to change because of pride, stubbornness, and an unwillingness to give up the things that they currently practice, even if it is going to change their life for the better. Other reasons for a person not making a life change is because they have a strong contentment with their existing sinful life or all of the above reasons rolled into one mindset. Worldly sorrow means that even though you cry or shed tears over the exposure of your sins and the heavy burdens and consequences that come with it, you are only crying because you were exposed or got caught in your sins, not because you wanted to turn away from your sins.

I remember years ago in the year 2001, when the following Sunday after the tragic events of 9-11 happened in New York City, many people came to the church I was attending at that time in Los Angeles and during the altar call, twenty-nine people came up to the altar to get saved. Those same twenty-nine people then got prayer from the altar workers and then were rotated to the baptismal pool to get water baptized in Jesus name. Then after this was complete, when the crisis was past where they were no longer fearful for their lives and when the mourning for their dead loved ones that died in the World Trade Center was completed, those same people left up out of the church house and went back to practicing what they were originally doing before 9-11 hit.

So in essence, 9-11 scared them into the church house through a spirit of fear. But once they got their temporary relief, believing it was safe to return to their normal activities and daily routines, no longer afraid that either they or their loved ones were in danger of dying anymore, they then left up out of the church house to return to their lives of self-will and spiritual leisure. The spirit of fear scared them into the church house, but the spirit of fear could not keep them in the church house! You cannot remain planted in the house of the Lord unless you are planted on the right foundations of godly sorrow that works repentance.

In evangelism, people's motives are called into question. Many people that exercise "worldly sorrow" and only want to go to church when it's convenient for them or when things get really bad for them. In these cases, they go to church in order to get prayer, healing and prophetic words spoken over them. In this way, they attempt to lay low for a week or two to get temporary relief from the consequences of their sins and their God-less lifestyle just before they run out to commit these same sins all over again. This is the natural outgrowth and outworking of worldly sorrow's fruit to cultivate an ungodly harvest. When people that exercise these examples of worldly sorrow continue to exhibit these reoccurring patterns of see-saw type behavior to go on in this state indefinitely, the end result is death without salvation. The principle of both a changed heart and a changed mind were never met since the person was operating in worldly sorrow which will always work death in mankind.

Remember that the evangelist does not come to condemn the world. The evangelist (through the agency of the Holy Ghost) comes to convict the world of its sinful course through the preaching of the gospel so that those lives that are being controlled by the world might reverse their course and be saved through the gospel. The difference between condemnation and conviction is that condemnation seeks to judge the world of its sins and place people into hell. Conviction comes to uproot and dislodge a person's comfort and contentment with living in sin so that they will ultimately be drawn to repentance and salvation. So when an evangelist preaches the gospel, the intention of that preaching is to convict a person of their sins so that they will repent and get saved. Love and compassion will convict a person in order to draw that person to Christ while bitterness, hatred, envy, jealousy, unforgiveness and other unloving behavior seeks to condemn a person and send them to hell. We must learn to lead with love!

Now if you see double-minded people coming into a church and leaving it just as quickly after their profession of wanting to receive salvation, then obviously those people were not serious about living for God and quite possibly that church didn't have a high level of discernment to ascertain what level of sorrow the people were actually manifesting.

Perhaps the gospel was not properly positioned to prick those people's hearts in order to generate the godly sorrow that is requisite for true repentance. Many altar workers do not even know the difference between godly sorrow and worldly sorrow because of a lack of prophetic insight, wisdom and discernment when they work the altar. In most cases, they simply look for a person to come forward with their hands raised up in the air thanking and praising God with a loud voice while they are worked up into an emotional state. They will also look for a person that comes forward crying and most of the time people's tears will satisfy the altar workers.

This is why altar workers need a strong impartation of prophetic wisdom and discernment if they are ever going to properly work the altar and correctly ascertain whether a person has really repented or not.

If you don't see people coming into the local church frequently with a changed mind and heart to get saved, then something may be wrong with that local church's evangelism, outreach strategies, improper positioning of the gospel or content of the gospel that they are preaching.

The Power of Repentance

Evangelism is not the practice of taking people that are already saved, grouping them into a denomination and then shuffling and recycling them from one church to another within that denomination in order to bolster and increase the congregational numbers for that particular local church. This is what I like to call "religious recycling". **Religious recycling is not true evangelism.** It is simply a religious shell game that many churches play when they are only concerned about increasing their congregational numbers in order to have the *appearance* of numerical growth when they really don't. There may be an alteration and even an increase in the numbers of the congregation, but that doesn't translate to the entrance (translation) of a soul coming into the Kingdom of God, which is the main priority. There is no poor man's substitute for salvation! You either have the genuine article or you don't have it at all.

Luke 15:7 tells us that there shall be joy in heaven over one sinner that comes to repentance, even more so than ninety-nine righteous persons that don't need repentance. This is a strong principle that we must learn. Just because you have 20,000 church members doesn't necessarily mean that heaven is rejoicing. We must first ascertain how many of those church members actually came to true repentance, true salvation, true deliverance and true empowerment and are walking in the fear of God *before* we get excited at our numbers. Numbers alone does not constitute success otherwise the judge Gideon would have kept his 32,000 plus men instead of whittling his numbers down to 300 when he went into battle. But the real question is, "What is the spiritual condition of those numbers?" That is the question.

God is concerned with quality over quantity and that is why heaven rejoices when only one soul comes to repentance.

This concept differs greatly than just having an increase in numbers because of the spiritual quality and fruit that is produced by one repentant soul. When someone brings forth fruits worthy of repentance, then that is precious in God's sight. Because during their repentance process, they will come forth confessing their sins. When a person confesses their sins, there is a strong deliverance element connected to it because they have become transparent about their way of life and want to change in order to have a better life.

When a person becomes honest with themselves, honest with God about themselves and honest to others about themselves, then these confessions of sin mixed with a heart of repentance are strong gateways to salvation.

This may not get the world or a lot of churches excited (although it should), but when we re-evaluate what heaven gets excited about and then properly align ourselves with what heaven considers worth rejoicing, then we will be in a better position to release God's perfect will in the earth realm that will be pleasing to Him.

But if we want to be worldly, we will overlook the importance of repentance at the expense of "just having larger numbers". When mindsets and lifestyles have not been delivered properly from worldly thought processes and patterns, then those people are still considered "worldly".

Jesus Christ said that we are in the world, but we are not of the world and that is why when an evangelist or any other minister of God gets ready to minister, they must first gain deliverance *from* the world so that they can effectively minister the gospel *to* the world.

Positioning Gospel Repentance

We cannot overlook the importance of repentance because repentance is powerful! **The call to repentance is also the call to count up the cost.** People that have truly repented have already counted up the cost of what salvation will require of them and will understand that salvation will cost them their lives. In other words, they will understand the price that they will have to pay that is needed to live for Christ. They will understand that they will have to stop walking in darkness and pursue after righteousness through a permanent lifestyle change and they will come to this understanding even before they are converted. Because when the gospel is properly positioned, people will understand prior to the completion of their salvation process that their walk with Christ will include future opposition, warfare and persecution that they will have to go through. Armed with this knowledge, they will still go through with the decision to get saved because they have successfully "crunched the numbers" and decided that the cost of salvation was still a price worth paying. Essentially, a person that repents and gets saved will already understand that they will have to suffer for the name of Christ.

And so in the final analysis, these people that get saved off of the hearing of the gospel that is *properly positioned* will more than likely finish their course with joy because they have already made up in their minds that they are ready to go all the way with God and not just when the sun is shining.

A person could be living like the devil for 60 years of their life, but once God leads them to repentance, they will do an immediate about-face and course correction in their mindset and lifestyle.

Through the preaching and the penetration of the gospel, human culture begins to be transformed.

People will change their mindsets, their way of life, their belief systems and their worldview because of the power of Christ that brings deliverance and enlightenment to human culture. When people's belief systems change, then their focus, their walk and their habits change.

Remember that it is the goodness of God (and not us) that leads a man to repentance. This is a very powerful principle that we must grasp because the concept of repentance, in and of itself, is a great miracle even before a person makes the transition after that into salvation. And the reason for this is because with repentance, a person's mind is made up that they are going to renounce how they have previously lived their life in order to live for God for the rest of their life. This is what makes the transition into salvation so much sweeter because the candidates in question are not double-minded or unstable in their ways, but they, with firm resolve, are passionate about wanting to live for God and are passionate about pursuing His greater purpose for their lives without looking back to wonder what they missed out on in the world.

If senior leaders of local churches would only get on one mind and one accord to properly position the gospel with an evangelistic focus of drawing souls to Christ through agape love instead of drawing church members through false promises, hype and smoke and mirrors, then their "church membership turnover rate" would sharply and dramatically decrease. How can you be a strong general or commander of the army of the Lord if you don't employ wise strategy to win the battle?

This is why the strategy of salvation in all cases calls for repentance to *precede* salvation if a person is going to ever get properly saved into the Kingdom of God.

When this strategy is implemented, it will sharply decrease the probability of these newly saved souls backsliding out of the house of God right back into the world.

But with proper gospel positioning and strategic preaching of the gospel, these newly saved souls are now ready to pay and endure the cost of the Kingdom. But the converse of Luke 15:7 is that if heaven is not rejoicing, it is because no souls ever came to repentance. No matter how many large numbers of people we invite to our local church houses, conferences, conventions, gospel cruises and our TV networks, heaven only looks at how many of those souls that took part in such events actually repented. No matter how good we sound or how good we preach, heaven only looks to see if our preaching was releasing the right Kingdom sound that would prick the people's hearts into a universal call to repentance. You see heaven knows the truth even if we don't! We must understand that evangelism is not for saved people. It is for the lost. And the lost are located in the world.

This is how you will know that true evangelism *manifests* by its fruit and not just its words!

THE FOUNDATIONS OF SALVATION

Origins of Salvation

Ever since Adam and Eve's fall in the Garden of Eden, mankind has always needed scapegoats and saviors in every dispensation and time period in earthly history subsequent to Eden. The reason for this is because every man or woman that is born on the face of this earth is born in sin and shaped in iniquity because of Adam and Eve's sin in the garden.

Therefore, at some point between birth and the grave, mankind must be born again in order to get back to the place of redemption, reconciliation and fellowship with God in order to re-enter His Kingdom and spend the rest of eternity with Him.

The Dialect of the Kingdom

Satan deals in complexity and convolution while God deals in simplicity and sincerity.

This is why the Apostle Paul said that his speech and his preaching did not come with enticing words of man's wisdom, but in the demonstration of the Spirit and power (dunamis). In other words, the Holy Spirit gave Paul the right words to speak so that those words would have the power to generate the results of Kingdom harvest. The reason for this is because Paul wasn't simply just a believer of Christ. He was disciple of Christ.

When it comes to preaching the gospel, less is more. We have to make it plain and crystal clear to all people what God is calling for and that is why when preaching the gospel before crowds, the language of the gospel must be accented with the dialect of the Kingdom of God so that it will produce ears that hear and obey the message of eternity.

When the preached message of the gospel has been properly *accented* with a Kingdom dialect, it will generate greater production from the messenger and greater harvest from the message.

Because the dialect of the Kingdom itself will tailor the gospel to have a universal impact on all people that come from all walks of life, family backgrounds, cultures and educational levels to give them a complete understanding of the Kingdom call to repentance and salvation in simplicity and sincerity.

A dialect is a special variety of a language. Dialects carry a certain pattern of speech sounds in a particular language.

You could have a person speaking with a Southern dialect that is common to many people that live in the southern part of the United States. This pattern of speech is easily recognizable when they speak. You could also recognize someone that lives in the Northeastern part of the United States simply by hearing the dialect that they speak by. New Yorkers and Bostonians have a distinct dialect that is unmistakable. Now we can also apply this principle of dialect recognition to other areas to properly ascertain the spiritual dialects that pertain to specific spiritual cultures.

The key to whether the gospel message will have a universal impact on all cultures is to see if the message of the gospel is preached by a messenger that carries the right dialect that will produce the right sound.

This is why the language and dialect of the Kingdom of God is radically distinct from the language and dialect of religion and man-made tradition.

When you take a person that has the dialect of religion (which originates from a religious spirit and is characterized by the sounds of man-made religious culture) and then have that person preach the gospel message, it will draw people of "like spirits", similar cultures and similar religious orientations to hear the message of the gospel from that particular messenger's mouth.

Certain preachers release dialects that draw specific races, ethnicities and cultures by the sound that they release and by the way that they preach while other preachers draw certain spirits (good or bad) by the spirit that they release when they preach.

So then the nature of the draw is dependent on the sound and the spirit that they are releasing when they preach the gospel message.

Birds of a feather will flock together and that is why religious spirits that preach the gospel will do so to draw like-minded and like-spirited crowds that will easily assimilate themselves into a self-righteous system of religion and tradition that's present at that preacher's local church. These people receive the word of God mixed with religion, but they are not receiving the unmixed word of God that is the by-product of an undiluted Kingdom. Religious spirits will continue preaching the gospel while simultaneously setting up environments that carry their same spiritual culture.

This is why before the evangelist begins their preaching discourse, they must first deliver themselves from any and all spiritual perversions so that they can have the freedom to release the true sound of the Kingdom by speaking with the correct Kingdom dialect.

When you take a messenger that speaks with the dialect of the Kingdom, they will preach that same message with a sound that is so distinct and so peculiar that it will draw a multi-cultural and multi-spiritual audience to hear and repent at the preaching of the gospel of God. The gospel is properly given to the universal masses because it was spoken by a strong Kingdom dialect. The Kingdom dialect will draw all people from all walks of life to come together in one place to hear the message. The dialect of the Kingdom enables evangelists to become the head and not the tail in their evangelism to draw people from all nationalities to sit at their feet so that the message of the gospel can touch their hearts and transform their lives to produce international impact and transformation.

Now you may be asking the question, "How can I know the difference between the Kingdom dialect and the dialect of man-made religion and tradition?" Another question you might ask is, "How can I preach the gospel with a Kingdom dialect?" Well I'm glad you asked those questions! God has reserved this dialect for those messengers who have undergone spiritual circumcision. This is not the natural circumcision of the male or female genitalia, but it is the spiritual circumcision of the heart and the spirit (Romans 2:29).

That way there is a clear distinction between someone who preaches the gospel by releasing the true sound of the Kingdom to produce the results of Kingdom harvest vs. someone who preaches the gospel, well versed in theology, specializing in the mechanics of preaching to release a religious spirit and emotionalism for the purpose of recruiting church membership to receive the praise of men.

The proof of this will manifest in either the abundance of Kingdom harvest or the absence of Kingdom harvest. The dialect of the Kingdom will draw people with specific hearts of readiness that will hear the gospel intently with the intention of obeying it to enter into the Kingdom. This is the difference between drawing a remnant of people into the kingdom of God that will readily enter into discipleship to do God's will vs. drawing people that only want to gain church membership, but don't want to go through the discipleship that will change and transform their lives because they still want to be in control of their own deliverance.

When messengers preach the gospel with only an earthly cultural dialect, they will tend to draw people that have the same dialects, motives and worship practices of that particular earthly culture to become unchanged church members (who may or may not be in the Kingdom of God) who are resistant to Kingdom discipleship.

These people will govern their lives and their worship by the culture of their race, city, region or nation, but won't govern their lives by the culture of the Kingdom.

But we have to understand that church membership, by itself, does not constitute Kingdom harvest. It has to be the right dialect that releases the right sound of the gospel that will produce the right Kingdom harvest.

If your preaching discourses cannot produce the right dialect that will, in turn, produce repentant people that are ready to progress into salvation and discipleship, then you must go back to the drawing board in your strategy and ministry of evangelism.

The Hearing Ear

Remember that the words of Christ are spirit and they are life, so in order for you to properly hear the words of Christ in its correct context with its intended meanings, you must be in the right spiritual place to properly hear them. Otherwise you will be spiritually deaf to the word of God and also deaf to your purpose in God. Because the serpent influenced Eve to listen to his voice and his words that both she and Adam would be as gods to have the ability to discern between good and evil if they ate the fruit, the satanic voice in her ear ultimately blinded and corrupted her mind from the simplicity of obeying God's one easy instruction to not eat from the tree of the knowledge of good and evil. It also caused Eve to become a carrier of this same demonic influence to carry this same seduction and sedition into her husband's ears so that he could also partake of the fruit to disobey God's original commandment, thereby sinning against God.

And because of this sin, Adam and Eve immediately died spiritually (and later on naturally) and got expelled from the garden so that they were no longer in fellowship and communion with God. They also could no longer remain in a spiritual position to hear God's voice of instruction. And now the rest of humanity subsequent to Adam and Eve's expulsion from Eden suffers from the same syndrome that Adam and Eve fell into: ears that do not hear the word of God.

Remember that the proper context for "hearing" the word of God is not to hear His word for informational purposes or for entertainment value, but to hear the word with the intention of obeying it from a humble and obedient heart.

This is why Jesus made the statement, "Let these sayings sink deep down into your ears" and this is why His admonition to the churches in the book of Revelation was, "he that has ears to hear, let him hear what the Spirit has to say to the church". Jesus knew how unregenerate mindsets think and how this thinking and ungodly stance can harden a person's heart and shut their ears to His word. So then the word of God must be strategically planted into a person's ear so that they can properly listen to the gospel and also understand the will of God since that preached word is accented with a Kingdom dialect.

Your comprehension of the will of God and the mind of Christ will come from your initial and progressive levels of hearing.

Proverbs 20:12 <u>The hearing ear, and the seeing eye, the LORD has made even both of them</u>.

This is a powerful scripture because it highlights the great need for ears that have the ability to hear the gospel and spiritual eyes that have the ability to see God's invisible Kingdom. It further implies that "seeing eyes" and "hearing ears" are not common to everyone. In the world system, these types of eyes and ears are not plentiful, nor are they in abundance. So then God has to "spiritually circumcise" your ears so that you can have the ability to properly *hear* the preaching of the gospel and also respond appropriately to it. If God has not opened your ears to hear His gospel, then you cannot properly respond to it even though you hear the natural sounds of the message of truth, redemption, deliverance and salvation being preached to you.

Remember that the preaching of the cross of Christ is foolishness to those that perish because the gospel cannot penetrate "uncircumcised ears" that are closed to God's will. When God "makes" an ear, he will plant this type of ear to have the ability to understand spiritual things and respond accordingly.

Only circumcised ears that truly have the ability to hear the voice of the Son of God can then transition their lives from a state of spiritual death to having eternal life.

Only circumcised ears will listen to the true message of the hour to save men's souls and enable the heart of a man to properly respond to its call. Our ears must be circumcised!

Itching Ears

Self-righteous, apostate, deceived, deluded and all other types of unbelieving people have what is known as "itching ears". This phrase refers to people that long for and look for preachers and teachers that will preach and teach them fleshly, watered down messages that they want to hear and not the godly types of messages that they need to hear. Itching ears want to hear stories and fables for the purposes of amusement and entertainment to warm their hearts in order to reinforce their own desires to live how they want to live. Just as people go to fittings to have clothing designers to design tailor-made suits to their exact specifications, so will itching ears run to find "tailor-made" preachers that preach fleshly messages that will line up to the exact specifications of their ears. This is why itching ears will always run to and throw money at "tailor-made" preachers.

Itching ears do not have the capacity or the desire to hear the truth of the gospel that fosters repentance and correction. Itching ears also don't have the capacity to endure any message that brings godly change and growth to their lives.

Itching ears will always lead people into stunted spiritual growth, underdevelopment, foolishness, confusion, error and great carnality.

Faith Comes By Hearing

Romans 10:16 But they have not all obeyed the gospel. For Isaiah says, Lord, who has believed our report?

Romans 10:17 So then faith comes by hearing, and hearing by the word of God.

When we look at the word "hearing", it is in reference to "giving reverent audience" to the preaching of the word of God. Hearing also means that we are listening with the intention of understanding and obeying the preached word. When we properly revere the word of God through the vehicle of the gospel, we will then allow that word to influence us into obeying it.

Whenever the gospel of the Kingdom is truly preached correctly to individuals, people, people groups and nations that have hearing ears, then the product of those ears that hear the gospel will produce strong hearts of faith and belief in Jesus Christ.

And belief's progression produces godly signs and wonders.

Mark 16:17 And these signs shall follow them that believe; In my name shall they cast out devils; they shall speak with new tongues;

Mark 16:18 They shall take up serpents; and if they drink any deadly thing, it shall not hurt them; they shall lay hands on the sick, and they shall recover.

Notice how belief's progression produces irrefutable signs of the Kingdom of God as the fruit of a person's steadfast and ongoing belief in God. Jesus Christ said that all things are possible to him that believes. And this is not a one-time belief.

This is a continual ongoing belief in God that produces progressive signs based off of a progressive faith. Belief is a powerful thing! But without belief, none of these things are possible. We must have faith to believe the gospel!

THE WAY OF SALVATION

The New Birth

When Jesus Christ hung upon the cross at Calvary and shed His blood for all the sins of mankind, He tore down the middle wall of partition to create an open door of access for all of mankind to receive salvation by the New Birth experience.

Mankind's access to God comes by the vehicle of Calvary which is facilitated through the womb of the Church. The Church is also called the Bride of Christ or the Body of Christ.

The New Birth is the great spiritual birthing process that every man and woman must experience if they want to enter into the Kingdom of God to live a greater life of glory and excellence through salvation.

Entrance into the Kingdom of God is absolutely essential to gaining access to the grace of God in order to go to heaven.

Remember that the grace of God that *brings* salvation has appeared to all men (Titus 2:11). But even though the grace of God has brought salvation into existence and availability, you must still make the choice to do what is required to *access* salvation. So how does one become born again? Let's give you the foundation first by examining a section of scripture in the book of St. John 3:1-8.

John 3:1 There was a man of the Pharisees, named Nicodemus, a ruler of the Jews:

John 3:2 The same came to Jesus by night, and said to him, Rabbi, we know that you are a teacher that has come from God: for no man can do these miracles that you do, except God be with him.

John 3:3 Jesus answered and said to him, **Assuredly, assuredly, I say to you, Except a man be born again, he cannot see the kingdom of God**.

Here Jesus is explaining to Nicodemus that he must be born again in order to be able to "see" the Kingdom of God. In other words, he is not saying that you will be able to see the Kingdom visibly with the natural eye since the Kingdom does not come with natural observation, but you will be able to see it with *spiritual* eyes once you become born again. This means that after the New Birth experience, you will be able to spiritually and cerebrally process the Kingdom way of life and also be able to think, speak, understand and walk the course of your life and destiny by Kingdom culture. This is what God commands and this is how we must walk.

Let's read further.

John 3:4 Nicodemus said unto him, How can a man be born when he is old? Can he enter the second time into his mother's womb, and be born?

Here Nicodemus does not understand what Jesus said or what He meant because he was still thinking with a natural, carnal mindset. As such, he was asking Him how could a man possibly be "naturally" born again and then begins to speak along that train of thought and earthly mindset by trying to speculate how a man can enter and exit his mother's womb a second time. This is why in verse five, Jesus must clarify and expound on what He meant earlier in verse three.

John 3:5 Jesus answered, Assuredly, assuredly, I say to you, **Except a man becomes born of water AND of the Spirit, he CANNOT enter into the kingdom of God**.

Here Jesus makes it plain to Nicodemus that the way of entrance into the Kingdom of God requires a person to be born of the water and born of the Spirit. This is the specific way of entrance that must be followed if a man or woman is ever going to be born again.

So then after reading this you may ask, "What does it mean to be born of the water and of the Spirit?"

To be "born of water" refers to water baptism. When referencing water baptism, we look at the Greek word "baptizo". When translated, it means that water baptism is **the act of submerging and immersing a person underwater *completely*** before they come back up again out of the water. If a person has not been submerged underwater completely, then their water baptism has not been properly and completely executed. The act of sprinkling water on someone does not constitute a valid baptism. And just in case you hear a teaching that states that the "water" is the "written word of God" and that being born of the water means to submerge yourself in the written word of God, that teaching is in error. This context of scripture does not indicate that the written word of God is the water. Now Ephesians 5:26 is talking about that context, but St. John 3:5 is talking about physical water. After the Church began in Acts chapter two, all New Testament water baptisms were administered in the name of Jesus Christ for the remission of a person's sins (Acts 2:38, Acts 8:16, Acts 10:48, Acts 19:5).

To be born of the Spirit refers to receiving the baptism of the Holy Spirit. When a person first receives the baptism of the Holy Spirit, there will be an initial sign of speaking in other tongues (languages) as the Spirit of God gives the utterance.

These are not languages that you have learned or have been taught by someone else, nor will you be speaking in your native tongue, but it will be languages that are birthed from the Spirit of God that you will speak out of your mouth once you are born of the Spirit.

A person can receive the baptism of the Holy Spirit four ways:

1. Tarrying (waiting) (Acts 1:4)

2. Hearing the word of the gospel (Acts 10:44)

3. The laying on of hands (Acts 8:17; Acts 19:6)

4. Prayer to God (Acts 8:15)

The common thread that ties all four of these vehicles together is a **heart of belief**. If you don't believe or have faith in Jesus Christ, then you will not receive the Spirit, no matter which vehicle is used. Belief is the primary catalyst that enables access to any of these four vehicles.

So to sum it up, when a person is truly born again according to the scriptures, they will:

1. **Believe the gospel**
2. **Repent of their sins and their former way of life**
3. **Be water baptized in the name of Jesus Christ (for the remission of their sins)**
4. **Be filled with the baptism of the Holy Ghost**

Following these 4 steps will *complete* any person's new birth process and also complete their entrance into the glorious Kingdom of God to experience a wonderful salvation. How marvelous!

We must understand that salvation does not exist outside of the Kingdom of God.

Many people think that they get saved by raising their right hand and repeating after a televangelist and then they will receive the Holy Ghost *after* salvation. This is not true and is a misnomer. Salvation only exists *within* the Kingdom of God, not outside of the Kingdom. A person cannot say "I am saved, but I'm just not born again yet" or "I'm saved, but I just don't have the Holy Ghost yet" or again, "I'm saved, but I just haven't entered the kingdom of God yet" and finally, "I'm saved, sanctified and then filled with the Holy Ghost". Salvation, redemption, being born again, the New Birth experience and gaining entrance into the Kingdom are all terms that are synonymous with each other and denote the same thing. As such, they are one in the same. It is not possible to do one without the other. You cannot be saved, sanctified and then filled with the Holy Ghost because the Holy Ghost *is* the sanctifier.

John 3:6 That which is born of the flesh is flesh; and that which is born of the Spirit is spirit.

John 3:7 Don't be astonished because I have told you, **You must be born again**.

Being born again is not an option. It is a command from our Lord and Savior and is a pre-requisite to coming into divine fellowship with God along with gaining citizenship within His Kingdom. When a person chooses not to become born again, they then continue to live their lives outside of the Kingdom of God (which means outside of salvation) because of disobedience to the command and therefore cannot please God since they have not obeyed His will.

John 3:8 The wind blows wherever it pleases, **and you hear the sound of it, but cannot tell where it comes from, and where it is going: so is every one that is born of the Spirit**.

This refers to the way that a person is born of the Spirit. A spirit is something that you can't see with the visible eye and can't track which direction it came from or which direction it is going. This is how a person is filled with the Holy Ghost because the Spirit is not coming from the natural realm of earth. He is coming from the spirit realm of heaven. The Holy Ghost enters into the earth realm and into a person audibly and experientially, but not visibly. What is notable about this is that the verse says "and you hear the sound of it". In other words, you can only hear the Holy Ghost, but you can't see the Holy Ghost. How can you hear the Holy Ghost? You hear Him by the tongues (languages) that are spoken from the individual receiving the Spirit. This is a prime example of something spiritual stepping into the natural realm to accomplish the will of the Father.

Once the Spirit has been received into a person, then that person can also give a word of prophecy that is inspired from the utterance of the Spirit. This is an announcement to both the individual and those that are around the individual that he/she has received the baptism of the Holy Spirit. The powerful thing about this is that these languages were not taught to the individual or learned by the individual, but it is simply the Holy Ghost speaking through the individual. This is the sound of the Kingdom! Hallelujah!

1st Century Salvations

Acts 2:1 And when the day of Pentecost had fully arrived, they were all gathered together with one accord in one place.

Acts 2:2 And suddenly there came a sound from heaven as of a rushing mighty wind, and it filled all the house where they were sitting.

Acts 2:3 And there appeared to them cloven tongues like as of fire, and it sat upon each of them.

Acts 2:4 And they were all filled with the Holy Ghost, and began to speak with other tongues, as the Spirit gave them utterance.

Acts 2:37 Now when they heard this, **they were pricked in their heart**, and said to Peter and to the rest of the apostles, Men and brethren, what shall we do?

The pricking of the heart lets us to know that the preaching of the gospel has penetrated the walls that people have raised and constructed around their hearts.

The reason for these walls could have been due to past hurts, trust issues, tragedies, backstabbing, betrayals, rejections, abandonments, molestations, demonization, etc. No matter what the issue is, when a sent one begins to preach the gospel with the authority of heaven to back them up, it has the power to break down every satanic wall of resistance in order to reach and prick the hearts of men. The gospel of the Kingdom is powerful!

Acts 2:38 Then Peter said to them, **Repent, and be baptized every one of you in the name of Jesus Christ for the remission of sins, and you shall receive the gift of the Holy Ghost**.

Notice that Peter is reiterating the same thing that Jesus told Nicodemus in St John 3:1-8. Peter, however, is making it plain that we must repent of our sins and former way of life, be water baptized in the name of Jesus Christ for the remission of our sins and then the Holy Ghost is *promised* to us. Notice that the scripture says that once a person is water baptized in Jesus name, they will then receive the full *remission* of their past sins. The word "remission" means "to release from bondage or imprisonment". It also means to "pardon" or "forgive" your lifelong sins, effectively erasing them from God's memory as though they had never been committed. God will throw all of your past sins into the sea of forgetfulness simply by you gaining *access* to the blood of Jesus Christ through the vehicle of water baptism.

When you are baptized into Christ, you have been baptized into his death (Romans 6:3-4) and by faith the blood of Jesus Christ cleanses you from all unrighteousness. Every sin that you have ever committed from the time you came out of your mother's womb to the time you got water baptized in Jesus name will be washed away forever! Remember that the servant is not greater than the master. Even as Jesus Christ naturally experienced His death, burial and resurrection, so must we also follow suit to *spiritually* experience His death, burial and resurrection.

Here's how:

1. **Death**-We die out to a sinful lifestyle by repenting of our sins and our former way of life.
2. **Burial**-Our past sins are buried and erased forevermore by water baptism and the blood of Jesus Christ.
3. **Resurrection**-we are resurrected into the newness of a changed and greater life by receiving the baptism of the Holy Spirit.

1 John 5:8 and 9 also says that there are three things that bear witness in the earth: the Spirit, the water, and the blood. These three witnesses agree in one. So when you have the witness of the Holy Spirit working on the inside of you, water baptism burying all of the past sins of your old man and lastly the blood of Jesus being applied to your life, then you will have all three witnesses testify that your salvation has been authenticated. The bible says that "in the mouth of two or three witnesses shall every word be established" (2 Corinthians 13:1). These three witnesses serve as irrefutable proof that you are saved. The witness of God is far greater than the witness of men!

Remember that salvation is free, but it will cost you your life.

Acts 2:41 <u>Then they that gladly received his word were baptized</u>: <u>and the same day there were added to them about three thousand souls</u>.

Notice that the 3,000 souls were added to the Kingdom of God only after they had been water baptized in Jesus name and received the gift of the Holy Ghost. But they never would have been baptized had they not gladly received the word. And you cannot gladly receive the life-changing gospel until your mind has been changed from its previous course. This is why people should not get water baptized until they have received the message of the gospel and want to change their minds to obey God's will for their souls to be saved.

Let's look at another biblical example of salvation.

Acts 10:44 While Peter yet spoke these words, the Holy Ghost fell on all them which heard the word.

Acts 10:45 And they of the circumcision which believed were astonished, as many as came with Peter, <u>because that on the Gentiles also was poured out the gift of the Holy Ghost</u>.

Acts 10:46 <u>For they heard them speak with tongues, and magnify God</u>. Then answered Peter,

Acts 10:47 <u>Can any man forbid water, that these should not be baptized, which have received the Holy Ghost as well as we?</u>

Acts 10:48 And he commanded them to be baptized in the name of the Lord. Then they prayed for him to stay a certain amount of days.

Here after Peter preaches the gospel to the house of Cornelius (Gentiles), people began to receive the gift of the Holy Ghost *before* they were baptized in the name of the Lord Jesus Christ. In this way, God is showing us that it really doesn't matter whether water baptism or Spirit baptism comes first so long as *both* are fulfilled.

And lastly, we will look at the account of how Paul witnesses to the disciples of John the Baptist and their subsequent salvation.

Acts 19:1 And it came to pass, that, while Apollos was at Corinth, Paul having passed through the upper coasts came to Ephesus: and finding certain disciples,

Acts 19:2 He said to them, **Have ye received the Holy Ghost since you believed?** And they said to him, We have not so much as heard whether there be any Holy Ghost.

Here we see that belief is the pre-requisite to receiving the Holy Ghost, however belief by itself was not enough to satisfy the Apostle Paul.

Acts 19:3 And he said to them, **to what then were ye baptized?** And they said, To John's baptism.

Acts 19:4 Then Paul said, John assuredly baptized with the baptism of repentance, saying to the people, that they should believe on him which should come after him, that is, on Christ Jesus.

Acts 19:5 <u>**When they heard this, they were baptized in the name of the Lord Jesus**</u>.

Acts 19:6 <u>**And when Paul had laid his hands upon them, the Holy Ghost came upon them; and they spoke with tongues, and prophesied**</u>.

What is interesting to note is that Paul did not leave the disciples alone until after they were water *and* Spirit baptized. Once all twelve of them were born again of the water and of the Spirit, Paul was satisfied that their salvation and entrance into the Kingdom of God was fully complete.

Profession vs. Confession

Many people may profess Christ and profess that they are in Christ with their mouths, but they deny Him in their works, their character and their nature.

The New Birth is how you become *identified* with Christ, which enables you to *confess* that Jesus Christ is Lord.

Identification is the proof of the profession of your faith and identification is also the witness of your confession. To profess something means that a person can make a statement that they *think* or *believe* to be true void of the personal witness or proof necessary to confirm it.

A person can profess to believe in something that they learned by secondhand information by listening to a message on the radio or by the consensus of popular majority opinion. But these things alone cannot be the proof of their profession. They will still need to gather the irrefutable proof that is necessary to enable them to properly confess what they believe. And this requisite proof is where false evangelism falls far short of the mark because it deceives you into believing that your profession of Christ is a confession of Christ simply by you reciting the words of Romans 10:9.

This is why confession is not simply what you say!

To confess something is to *testify* of its truth because the person in question has personally *witnessed* its truth. This personal witness is that truth coming alive in that person's life to become their own life *experience*.

In a court of law, you cannot testify to a heinous act someone committed or an event that occurred if you never personally saw it happen. Consequently, you will not be a credible witness to the judge or the jury because what you only profess does not give you the ability to render proper testimony. So then the jury will not be able to factor in your "profession" as proper testimony in their decision-making process of pronouncing a "guilty" or "not guilty" verdict. Because your professed words of what you think you saw does not qualify as proper testimony that is needed to qualify as evidence that is necessary for a judge and jury to convict that person of their heinous act. Only if you personally saw it happen can the jury then conclude that you have rendered proper testimony and then factor in your testimony in their decision-making process. When you become a *personal witness* to a matter, then and only then can you testify to give personal confirmation to its validity.

This is why the word of God says that no man can testify that Jesus Christ is Lord, except by the Holy Ghost. By giving testimony to the Lordship of Jesus Christ, people in essence, are rendering their confession of His Lordship because they have personally witnessed this Lordship in their own lives.

So when you *confess* that God raised Jesus from the dead, you cannot be a natural witness to it since you cannot see God with the natural eye and because you were not around to be an eye-witness of the resurrection event that happened almost 2,000 years ago. But you can be a *spiritual* witness to its event by experiencing this same spiritual resurrection in your own life through the baptism of the Holy Ghost.

Once you receive the Spirit of God, your profession of Christ's resurrection can now be changed to a confession of His resurrection because you, by experience, have now become a living witness to the authenticity of this event.

This is why people that don't have the Holy Ghost can only profess Romans 10:9, but can't properly confess it because they haven't *personally* witnessed Christ's resurrection and therefore Jesus cannot be their personal Lord and Savior. If there is no personal witness, then their words of Christ's resurrection and His Lordship are reduced to a profession and not a confession because first, they cannot confess Christ's resurrection since He doesn't live on the inside of them and second, they cannot confess His Lordship because they are not living for Him.

And the tragic thing is that we have evangelism teams all across the earth that have a real passion and a real zeal for Christ, but because they lack understanding, their zeal is not being governed according to the knowledge of God. They are teaching people the wrong way on how to be saved and so, in essence, the sum total of their evangelistic efforts are seen as false evangelism because they themselves are not true witnesses of Christ (which means they are not saved). How embarrassing and humiliating that would be for an evangelism team to go out to evangelize the world only to discover that they themselves need to first be saved!

You cannot compel the lost to come into the Lord's Kingdom unless you have first personally entered and partaken of His Kingdom.

You can believe that Jesus is Lord, you can have a passion and a zeal for soul-winning and you can also have good intentions towards people, but unless you have the wisdom and knowledge of Christ on how to properly preach what a person needs to do to become saved, and are living what you are preaching, then all your efforts will be rendered as false evangelism.

But when your life becomes a living witness to the Lordship of Jesus Christ because of the New Birth experience and the fruit of its corresponding lifestyle, then and only then can you properly confess that Jesus Christ is Lord because He is personally Lord over your own life. This is why the principles of confession are far weightier than just simple profession! Professors of Christ can always make grand theological statements about God, but their messages will always lack credibility due to their own *inexperience* with God. A confessor will never sit at the feet of a professor because while professors think they know what they are talking about, confessors know for sure what they are talking about!

A professor thinks in terms of theory and theoretical application while a confessor speaks in terms of experience and experiential wisdom and "hands-on" knowledge, which opens the door to render strong testimonies of Christ to the masses. Theology without experience will always open the door to a mindset of doubt and a heart of unbelief that will tarnish a person's profession and ruin their credibility, especially when the winds of adversity come to test and try that person's belief systems.

This is why we must renounce the former teachings of doctrinal error that only condition our minds to embrace false methods and mindsets concerning salvation, whose fruit only produces false witnesses of Christ who are only outsiders looking in. Instead, we must lay the true foundational belief systems founded upon God's Word that will stand the tests and trials of adversity in order to strengthen our godly beliefs and proper confessions of Christ. Do you want to be a professor of Christ or do you want to be a confessor of Christ? Let's make the transition from profession to confession!

True Witness vs. False Witness

A false witness will only have the ability to profess Christ, but not have the ability to truly confess Christ.

A true witness of Christ will have the divine grace and ability to properly profess *and* confess Christ.

Furthermore, a true witness of Christ will have the ability to hold fast to the profession of their faith and also hold fast to the confession of their salvation. So it's either all or nothing. Your credibility in Christ and your credibility to the people that you minister to in the world, will only come by your *true* confession! You cannot be a true witness of Christ unless you have the divine grace and ability to properly confess Christ. Even as the word of God says that if Christ is not raised (resurrection), then we are not raised and ultimately we are made false witnesses of Christ if there be no resurrection of the dead (1 Corinthians 15:14-15). Now if Christ is resurrected, but you have not become a partaker of His resurrection by receiving the baptism of the Holy Ghost, then by you going around trying to evangelize people, you are in essence a false witness to something that you believe, <u>but have never experienced</u>.

Belief alone without a Christ-experience constitutes a false witness.

You may have the passion to win souls for Christ, but you must first check to see if you are in Christ. You must gain the divine power necessary to execute that passion of soul-winning with heaven's seal of approval in credibility and excellence. Evangelism cannot truly succeed through a false witness, nor can its fruit manifest if its messengers are false witnesses. If people cannot see the Christ in you or the fruit of the Holy Spirit manifest from your life and ministry example, then they will never be attracted to the light of Christ through your testimony since your "testimony" has been tarnished by a corrupted witness.

When the world sees any messenger of the gospel present a corrupted witness of Christ, then they will not see the true image or light of Christ in that messenger because the testimony itself has been soiled by a representative that walks in darkness.

Consequently they will not receive your message nor will they trust your ministry simply because they don't trust the false witness of an unfruitful messenger.

False evangelists are messengers that preach Christ, but they preach Christ from a position of association and not from a position of identification.

In other words, they are associated with Christ, but they are not identified with Christ. They are really outsiders looking in, but pretend to already be in. And this is dangerous because this can open the door for other ministers of unrighteousness to come in and preach Christ from a spirit of envy, strife and contention which is not the fruit of the Holy Spirit and is not the proper portrait of Christ.

When this happens, the gospel will be preached in great pretense and constant hypocrisy.

False evangelists can also be messengers that got saved, but have now become backslidden through an unholy lifestyle and are presenting a false spiritual witness to the masses when they preach even though the content of their preaching may be 100% correct.

But by receiving the baptism of the Holy Ghost and allowing your life to be led by the Holy Ghost, it will then enable you to become a true witness of Christ's resurrection since that resurrection lives on the inside of you and is manifesting its corresponding fruit through the vehicle of strong discipleship. How glorious!

THE PROGRESSION OF SALVATION

The Clarification of Romans 10:9

As we begin this portion of the book and this particular discourse, I want to preface this by saying that I am about to go through some tedious exposition. I am doing this because there has been a great misunderstanding and promotion of error on how a person experiences salvation due to a lot of doctrinal errors that have been taught in the exposition of soteriology (the doctrine of salvation through Jesus Christ). Furthermore, there has been much error in the improper positioning of the gospel of the Kingdom by the Body of Christ on a global scale due to a lack of prophetic strategy, a lack of revelation and the promotion of man-made traditions being mixed with the Word of God. These traditions and unholy mixtures don't line up with the Holy scriptures and they attempt to evangelize the world in our own strength without involving grace. What I am about to say, I say it in all agape love and want nothing but the best for those that profess Christ. But before we can experience the best that God has to offer us, we must first rectify the things that are in error and are lacking.

Now let us begin.

It has been widely promoted and accepted all across modern-day Christianity that all a sinner has to do in order to become a saint is to recite or quote Romans 10:9 and then they will be saved. This means that this prevailing thought has convinced the majority of the masses of humanity that by doing this recitation, they have fulfilled all the requisites and requirements of salvation including the New Birth born again experience.

This scripture says:

Romans 10:9 That if you shall confess with your mouth the Lord Jesus, and shall believe in your heart that God has raised him from the dead, you shall be saved.

On many religious TV and radio programs as well as many churches all around the world, many conductors of this practice often make various modifications to personalize this scripture for the viewing and listening audience by having them repeat a group of words that the host specifically has them recite based off of the Romans 10:9 scripture.

An example of this recitation (but not limited to this) may be:

"Repeat after me: Lord Jesus I acknowledge that you are Lord. I acknowledge my former sins and I believe that you went to Calvary and died for me. I accept that you are my personal Lord and Savior and I confess with my mouth and I believe in my heart that God raised you on the third day and I receive you into my heart this day. Amen."

The viewing or listening audience does as they are told and repeat these words. After they have finished reciting what the host wanted them to say, the host then pronounces them born again or saved at that very moment. After believing that they are saved, the viewing/listening audience or congregation then goes out to rejoice greatly in this deception, falsely assured that their status in eternity has changed.

But unfortunately, this "popular method" of salvation for a sinner to become a saint is not a true method of salvation that was practiced by the early church.

As a result of this error, this erroneous method of salvation has been a gross misnomer and a huge false evangelism tactic that has deceived millions of people and has also prevailed greatly in many churches, denominations and religious organizations worldwide. In reality, this method doesn't require you to be identified with Christ (even though they advertise it that way). It only requires you to be *associated* with Christ.

So then we must understand that true evangelism requires you to be identified with Christ, but false evangelism only wants you to be associated with Christ.

If you are only associated with Christ, then you are limited to only securing the blessings of Christ through your partnership with another person who is actually identified with Christ. But what happens when that partner is not available to assist you or meet up with you? Can you stand in God alone to be a Kingdom distribution center to dispense the blessings of Abraham to the world by your *association* with Christ? Not likely.

So then being blessed by association may put you into a temporary place of blessing, but ultimately it will put you into a permanent place of limitation.

Salvation is positioned to the masses in such a way that you must *accept* Jesus without actually repenting. When we look at the word "accept", it means "to agree to" or "to consent to". But if we look through the word of God, the gospel was never positioned for mankind to just simply accept Jesus because we are not in the position to accept God. Rather, it is positioned in such a way where a person must repent of their former mindset and former way of life in order to enter into salvation. Remember that God is in the position of headship, not us. And it is the one that is in the position of headship that does the accepting. So then it is God who *accepts us* if we do what is right, not the other way around. Our responsibility is to repent and believe the gospel so that we can access salvation to gain God's acceptance into His Body.

And what is being espoused to the world is the belief that mankind can enter into salvation without bringing forth the fruits of repentance. Consequently, as a result of this erroneous positioning of the gospel, these souls never enter into the Kingdom of God because the prior condition of repentance before salvation was never truly met. When we truly repent, we can now gain access to salvation because we have reversed our thought process and our way of life to embrace the New Birth.

The reason that this false popular method of salvation has prevailed is because people have not studied their bibles thoroughly enough to rightly divide the word of truth, but instead have become dependent on people telling them what they need to do or what they need to believe rather than seeing if what was taught to them lines up with the written Word of God in its proper context. We must understand why the Apostle Paul said what he said to the church at Rome. But before that, we must first understand the church at Rome's spiritual state. Every epistle from Romans to Jude is addressing an audience of people that are already saved *before* the epistle is even written.

So in the book of Romans, Paul is actually addressing a group of people that were *already* in the Body of Christ.

The book of Acts (which precedes the book of Romans in biblical order and chronology) is not simply just a history book, but it shows us how sinners got saved during the dispensation of grace (which we are still in to this present day). And every epistle of the New Testament is addressing people that have already made the spiritual transition from sinner to saint.

Once we understand this, our interpretation of Romans 10:9 will take on a different understanding than what was previously believed.

Let us look at Romans 1:7 which is Paul's opening address and salutation to the church at Rome.

Romans 1:6 Among whom you are also the called of Jesus Christ:

Romans 1:7 To all that be in Rome, **beloved of God, called to be saints**: Grace to you and peace from God our Father, and the Lord Jesus Christ.

Romans 1:8 First, I thank my God through Jesus Christ for you all, that **your faith is spoken of throughout the whole world**.

Notice that in these three verses of scripture, Paul is making it clear that he is addressing an audience that has already partaken of the New Birth experience. In verse six, he speaks of this group being the "called" of Jesus Christ and in verse seven he refers to them as the "beloved". In order to completely understand this, we must look at another scripture in order to go line upon line and precept upon precept. Ephesians 1:6 says that God has made us "accepted in the beloved".

"Beloved" is a term that indicates God's Body or His Bride. When you are in the Body of Christ, you have been accepted into the beloved of God.

This means you are saved. Furthermore verse seven of Romans chapter one indicates that the audience that Paul is addressing is "called to be saints".

Along with verse eight's indication that the church at Rome's faith was being spoken of throughout the whole world, these are clear cut indicators that Paul is not addressing a group of sinners at Rome. Sinners would not display this type of growth or progression in Christ because they are not yet saved. They would still be knocking on the door trying to get in. But rather, Paul is addressing a group of people that are already saints. We've already learned that in order for you to be considered a saint, you must first be saved.

Let's look at another three verses from the same chapter.

Romans 1:11 For I long to see you, **that I may impart to you some spiritual gift, to the end that you may be established;**

Notice that verse eleven speaks of Paul wanting to come to impart a spiritual gift so that the church at Rome can be strengthened and established. To "impart" means to "give" or "bestow". He is not speaking of laying hands on them that they would receive the baptism of the Holy Ghost. He is speaking of giving or bestowing an activation of a spiritual gift that comes from the Holy Ghost that is already on the inside of them. The reasons for this is for the purposes of establishing them in their Christian walk, fostering their spiritual growth, and cultivating fruit that will launch them into their life's purpose so that they can completely fulfill their destiny in God.

Romans 1:12 That is, that I may be comforted together with you **by the mutual faith both of you and me**.

"Mutual faith" is the key phrase here which indicates the same beliefs or convictions of both Paul and the church at Rome. Both parties could not be on one mind and one accord with the same belief systems and convictions when one party is saved and the other is not. The carnal mindset of a sinner and the spiritual mindset of a saint are two different animals that walk in two different directions. So then Paul is expressing to the Romans that he and they both share a common faith (Titus 1:4).

Romans 1:13 Now I would not have you ignorant, **brethren**, that many times I planned to come to you, (but have been prevented from doing so until now) **that I might have a harvest among you also**, even as I had a harvest among other Gentiles.

Paul is expecting fruit and harvest from his "brethren". But why would Paul have the expectation of seeing the fruit of the Spirit in a group of sinners who don't have the Holy Spirit? Not possible. He would only have that expectation from a group of saints that already have the Spirit. If these people were unsaved, his position would be to evangelize them in order to get them saved (as he did in Acts chapter 19 with the disciples of John the Baptist), not tell them how to grow and progress in Christ. **Instructions for growth and progression are reserved for people who are already in Christ.**

Now let us return to chapter ten of the book of Romans where we examine the nature of why Paul said what he said in verse nine.

Paul was telling the church at Rome that had Roman citizenship his desire for Israel to be saved.

Since Israel as a whole rejected Jesus Christ as their Messiah, Lord and Savior, they had a veil over their hearts that effectively blinded them to receiving the truth. Because of their hard and impenetrable hearts, their hearts and minds were rooted in steadfast unbelief. Unbelief has the opposite work of faith and this is why Paul is emphasizing the great need for the word of faith to be promoted, cultivated and spread among unbelieving Jews and Gentiles so that their stony hearts of unbelief will turn into hearts of faith.

As belief begins to take root in a person's heart, they will then make a strong profession of Christ which will ultimately lead to their mouth rendering a strong confession once they gain the proper witness. But remember that in order for you to "confess" a thing, you must first be a "witness" of that thing. You can profess a thing, meaning that you "think" that Jesus is Lord, but you cannot "confess" that He is Lord or that God raised Him from the dead except you first be a witness of His resurrection.

In order for you to become a witness of His resurrection, you must first have the baptism of the Holy Ghost (which is the Spirit that resurrected Jesus).

Once that same Spirit that raised up Jesus also raises you (through the baptism of the Holy Ghost), then you can properly confess with your mouth as well as testify with blessed assurance that God raised Him from the dead and that Jesus Christ is Lord. You are now fully persuaded of His resurrection by your confession because that same resurrection that raised Jesus *also* raised you!

The Progression of Salvation

So then with our new understanding, let us return to the book of Acts to see how belief catapulted the Philippian jailer and his entire house into their salvation.

Acts 16:30 And brought them out, and said, <u>Sirs, what must I do to be saved?</u>

Acts 16:31 And they said, **Believe on the Lord Jesus Christ, and you and your house shall be saved**.

Acts 16:32 <u>And they spoke to him the word of the Lord, and to all that were in his house.</u>

Acts 16:33 And he took them the same hour of the night, and washed their stripes; **and he and all his household were baptized immediately**.

Notice the progression here. The Philippian jailer asks what he must do to be saved. Paul and Silas tell him to believe on the Lord Jesus Christ and then he and his household would be saved. But watch the progression of the steps that would eventually result in the jailer's salvation.

1. He asked for salvation
2. He was told to believe on the Lord Jesus Christ
3. He listened to the word of the Lord that was preached to him first which sparked his belief in Christ
4. Later on during that same hour of the night he and his household were water baptized *because* of their belief

One of the strongest principles of evangelism lies in its *progression*.

There must be a progression of events that happens first before a person can complete their salvation. In other words, there is a progression of events that *produces* the heart of belief that is necessary to catapult a person towards their salvation. The main catalyst that produces belief in a person's heart is the preaching of the gospel and then the hearing of the gospel. Remember that faith comes by hearing and hearing by the word of God (Romans 10:17).

Now let's look further at the progression of salvation.

Romans 10:14 How then shall they call on him in whom they have not believed? and how shall they believe in him of whom they have not heard? and how shall they hear without a preacher?

Romans 10:15 And how shall they preach, except they be sent? as it is written, How beautiful are the feet of them that preach the gospel of peace, and bring glad tidings of good things!

This is why it must be stressed again that there is a progression of events that must unfold that will ultimately lead up to the completion of a person's salvation. Remember that you can't call on the Lord if you don't believe and you can't believe on the Lord unless you have heard the gospel. And you can't hear the gospel unless you have a preacher. And that preacher can't preach unless he/she is sent by God. And if belief has not been produced in the hearts of the people by the preaching of the gospel, then you will be wasting water if you baptize them. Nor will they receive the baptism of the Holy Spirit if they have hearts of unbelief.

In fact, a person cannot receive the Holy Spirit until the very moment that belief has been produced in a person's heart.

And *proper* belief in Jesus Christ cannot be produced in a person's heart unless they hear the right message from heaven. So bear in mind that the principle here is progression. There is progression in our preaching discourse of the gospel that produces a harvest of repentance and belief in the hearts and minds of our target audience.

Furthermore, as the word is sown into their hearts and minds, it will also begin to produce a harvest of *obedience* to the gospel and also obedience to the faith (Romans 1:5) as the outgrowth of the progression of a person's belief. And this progression of evangelistic harvest must be produced in the people's hearts after the messenger renders the gospel to the target audience. Belief, repentance *and* obedience to the gospel are the three things that must be produced in the heart of the sinner in order to progress and propel them towards the position of becoming a saint.

Precept Upon Precept

Then after the person has made the transition to salvation, they have now become a babe in Christ. From here, there is more progression involved for a babe in Christ to become a full grown adult in Christ.

This entails going from a position of desiring the sincere milk of the Word of God so that they can grow thereby to then progressing to the position of having the ability to digest strong meat. But in order to accomplish this growth, we must first experience progression.

If we stop our progression at just our initial belief that Jesus is Lord, then we will never come to the fullness of what is promised to us in the Word of God.

This is why belief by itself does not translate to identification with Christ. He that believes and is baptized shall be saved (Mark 16:16) because your progressive belief will transition you to water and Spirit baptisms. That is the progression that the Lord desires. This principle of progression dovetails nicely with the concept of one precept building upon the foundation of another precept.

Isaiah 28:10 <u>For precept must be upon precept, precept upon precept; line upon line, line upon line; here a little, and there a little</u>:

A precept is a commandment or a direction given as a rule of action or conduct.

One precept of God's Word will lay the foundation for other precepts to become strong building blocks to be built on top of the initial foundational precept.

This is why we cannot isolate Romans 10:9 from the rest of the scriptures to create a doctrine of salvation based on that one scripture alone because that would defeat the very purpose of cross-referencing that one verse with other pertinent verses that form a larger relationship designed to achieve interpretive balance. This also helps us to rightly divide the word of truth so that our interpretations of the Word of God, including all of its lines and precepts, come into perfect harmony and agreement with the mind of Christ.

Modes of Salvation

There are three modes or stages of salvation. They are:

1. **Relative Perfection** (Colossians 2:13)-This is where a sinner first gets saved through the New Birth experience to become a saint. They have relative perfection because the blood of Jesus has cleansed them of all of their past sins so that they start out with a clean slate. All of their past sins have been thrown into the sea of forgetfulness and God cannot judge them on any of their past sins because those sins will never come to His remembrance. Relative perfection means that we are not perfect in ourselves, but we are only relatively perfect because the blood of Jesus Christ has been applied to our lives and because we are in Christ who is perfect. We will still need to yield to the processes of perfection (maturation) in the next stage of salvation.

2. **Progressive Sanctification** (2 Thessalonians 2:13)- Here is the bulk of a person's salvation on earth as they occupy until Jesus comes back. This is also the largest time period of a saved person's earthly life as they work out their own salvation with reverent fear. During this time period, a saint will yield to the sanctification process of the word of God and the Holy Spirit as well

as go through different levels of progressive belief and faith in the truth of God. They will go through the sufferings of Christ that will ultimately process them into perfection (maturity). They will go through deliverance processes of renewing their minds so that they can serve God to a greater capacity in order to fulfill His divine, perfect will. The gifts of the Spirit and the fruit of the Spirit will be cultivated out of a person's life so that they can perform their God-assigned tasks and stewardships in excellence. They will grow in grace and go from the milk of the Word to being able to digest strong meat. If we happen to commit any sins out of omission, ignorance or willful disobedience, we have an advocate with the Father and the blood of Jesus will cleanse us of all the unrighteousness of our present sins just as soon as we come back to the place of confessing these sins followed by repentance.

There is great growth and progression in this stage of salvation because this is the process whereby a saint begins to perfect themselves through a powerful walk of self-discovery by receiving their identity, purpose and destiny to walk with God to higher levels and greater degrees of excellence and glory. Furthermore, they go through stages of empowerment and levels of progressive deliverance in Christ through the vehicle of spiritual processing. In essence, the believer goes through strong progressive periods of discipleship.

3. **Rewards Of Salvation** (1 Peter 1:9)-In this stage of salvation, we have come to the completion and culmination of our salvation. We first experienced the New Birth to have relative perfection. Next, we went through progressive periods of sanctification and lastly, we come to the end of our faith which is to receive the

salvation of our souls into heaven. Once we have arrived into heaven, we will receive the rewards of our enduring faith. Once a person comes to this stage of salvation, there is no possibility of them ever losing their salvation for the rest of eternity. One reward that comes into visible manifestation is the actual experience of eternal life played out over eternity. Another reward is God giving us glorified bodies that we will wear throughout eternity (2 Corinthians 5:1-4). Other rewards are specific crowns that God will award us depending on the righteous deeds that you did in your body during your godly stewardship over your earthly lifetime.

1 Corinthians 9:24 Do you not know that they which run in a race run all, but only one receives the prize? **So run, that you may obtain**.

1 Corinthians 9:25 And every man that strives for the mastery is temperate in all things. **Now they do it to obtain a corruptible crown; but we do it to obtain an incorruptible crown**.

2 Timothy 2:5 And if a man also strive for masteries, **he will not be crowned except he strive lawfully**.

So after *completing* mastery in your salvation walk, you may receive any or all of these incorruptible crowns:

A. Crown of Life (James 1:12; Revelation 2:10)

B. Crown of Righteousness (2 Timothy 4:8)

C. Crown of Glory (1 Peter 5:4)

These crowns are only promised to those that *abide* in Christ after their New Birth experience to then complete all of their processes and perfections of discipleship, hence mastery. These saved people do not depart from the Lord (backslide) so that at the end of their stay on earth, they can then be translated into heaven to receive their great rewards of godly service. If a person backslides, they then forfeit their crowns and their souls unless they come back to the place of repentance and reclamation to return back into the ranks of the redeemed. If a person gets reclaimed back to the Lord after previously backsliding, they will start out again with a clean slate not needing another water baptism, but they will have forfeited their crowns that they accrued prior to backsliding. This is due to the fact that their works have been burnt up and therefore they must start all over again earning their rewards of faith (1 Corinthians 3:12-15).

As we close this discourse on salvation's progression and this section of Forming The Net, I would like to leave you with an easy way to condense everything you read in this chapter pertaining to Modes of Salvation. We *begin* our salvation by Acts 2:38, we *progress* in our salvation living by grace through faith according to Ephesians 2:8 and Romans 10:9, and finally, we *culminate* our salvation at the end of our faith according to 1 Peter 1:9 to receive our rewards of godly service.

In other words, we first get saved, we continue being saved and at our future end, we will be saved. Amen.

WASHING THE NET

KINGDOM WASHING

Whenever fishermen finish a long day of fishing, the first thing they do after removing the catch from their nets is to wash those nets. This is the act of cleansing the nets from the smell and residue of an old catch so that later on the net can be used again to catch new groups of fish. This is very important to fishermen because once the net is re-deployed into the waters to catch new fish, the different and diverse types of fish that fishermen may want to attract to their nets may not come if the lingering residue of an old catch still remains. And not only that, but one dirty net that has been grouped with other clean nets will corrupt and contaminate the other clean nets that may be ready for deployment.

The Residue Of The Old Catch

Luke 5:1 And it came to pass, that, as the people pressed upon him to hear the word of God, he stood by the lake of Gennesaret,

Luke 5:2 And saw two ships standing by the lake: but the fishermen had left out of them, **and were washing their nets.**

Even so, when evangelists become fishers of men and deploy certain evangelistic strategies into the sea of mankind (the world), the strategy implemented will only work for that particular target group of people at that particular place and time.

A net is symbolic of the evangelistic strategy that you will be using to harvest souls from the world into the Kingdom of God. When a net is used in the plural sense, nets are then symbolic of using two or more strategies, usually to catch a larger harvest.

Nets also indicate the specific revelatory strategies which you must implement in your evangelism in order to properly secure the totality of the harvest of souls that are located in specific places, people groups or industries.

In order for an evangelistic team to continue to be effective in their evangelistic strategy, they must continually revise their strategies when speaking to different and diverse people groups. One people group can be sports athletes or entertainers while another group could be public officials that work for the government. A third group can be business professionals that work in the marketplace. So then our strategy for reeling in souls from the government sector of society may be radically different from our strategy of reeling in souls that work and do business in the marketplace.

Implementing Godly Wisdom

Proverbs 10:30 ....and he that wins souls is wise.

Remember that the Word of God says that he that wins souls is wise. So if we are ever going to constantly be successful in our soul-winning, we cannot work or labor in our own wisdom. We must win souls to Christ utilizing the wisdom of God.

This is why there must always be a constant revision of our approach and strategy when encountering different types of people working in different professions. There is a great wisdom in this because a government official may have one train of thought that formulates their mindset and the business professional may have a different train of thought that formulates a different mindset. If you preach the gospel with the same strategy to both people groups, then you will either succeed in winning only one of the groups or none of them at all. But if you want to win each person and each group of people that God sends you to evangelize, then you must implement the wisdom of God in your decision making and strategy.

The wisdom of God should dominate your entire thought process. Winning souls is not about how good you preach, how much bible you can quote or how much Greek or Hebrew you know. It is about "how" you render what you know utilizing God's revealed strategy at that given moment. Revelatory strategies are only good to us so long as we implement it, but they will be of no use to us if we are not obedient to use them.

Our greatest successes in evangelism will come with how well we carefully positioned the good news and how strategically we rendered the gospel.

The wisdom of God is the principal thing. So in essence, you must wash away your own thought processes, your traditional methodologies and your own way of thinking to renew your mindset for a better strategy. This is what must first take place in order for you to be in the right place spiritually to position your nets properly so that you can reel in the tremendous harvest that God has waiting for you!

This is why we must always be forever flexible in our strategy if we want to be able to effectively preach the gospel to every creature.

Sometimes you cannot go into the marketplace using a church title (apostle, prophet, bishop, evangelist, etc.) and then expect people to listen to you preach the gospel. Perhaps going in with just your name and no title in front of your name will be the more correct orientation and business protocol that is needed in professional business environments in order to gain better credibility with business professionals. This strategy is used for the purposes of strategically positioning yourself in the right areas of access in order to penetrate the marketplace with the gospel of the Kingdom using revised strategies from heaven. How many nets will you need to use in the marketplace? How, when and where will you need to deploy them?

Consecration and prayer will put you in a place to hear the voice of the Lord to correctly ascertain the precise amount of nets that will be needed to catch the numbers of souls that are waiting on your ministry to impact and transform them.

The gospel of the Kingdom will always work in every case as long as it is positioned and deployed correctly.

Forsaking Traditional Methodologies

The keys to becoming more relatable to your target audience lay in your faithfulness and your obedience to implement God's revelatory strategies and methodologies in your evangelism. Please understand that if you try to go out and win souls to the Lord in your own strength, you will not win a single soul to Christ. You may be able to convince them to visit or become a member of your church by using your own strength, but you will not succeed in winning them to the Kingdom of God. Strategy is what's key! You may have used one strategy to catch a group of fish in one part of the sea, but the next day you go out to fish, you cannot go to that same spot and then expect to reel in the same catch. Because the fish may have migrated to a different part of the sea and may not fall for the same bait that you put on your fishing hook the previous day.

So then the principle is that you cannot relate to or impact a 21st century audience if you are using a 20th century strategy and methodology.

Yesteryear's successful strategy is today's failed attempt! The strategy that worked 40 years ago has no chance of working today. Therefore, you must get new instructions from the throne of God through much prayer and fasting, which means that before you get those instructions, you will have to erase your former blueprint of evangelistic success and then replace it with a *present* blueprint that will come from heaven through prayer and prophetic wisdom.

Luke 5:37 <u>And no man puts new wine into old bottles; or else the new wine will burst the bottles, and be spilled, and the bottles shall perish</u>.

Luke 5:38 <u>But new wine must be put into new bottles so that both are preserved</u>.

Remember that new wine cannot be placed into old wineskins because old wineskins are hard, rigid and inflexible and therefore cannot expand their capacities to receive new revelation, new blueprints, new paradigms or new models of ministry. New wine can only be put into new wineskins because new wineskins have the flexibility to expand and the capacity to contain and house the total volume of the new wine without bursting. Existing wineskins must be *reformed* before new wine can be *restored*. Therefore in your ministry, reformation must precede restoration. The problem with modern day ministry is that we have prayed for new wine, but we haven't prayed for new wineskins. We must first pray for new wineskins so that we can be in prophetic position to receive the new wine.

So then your prayer mandates must carefully balance the need for new wine (present movements of God's Spirit) with the petition for new wineskins (new paradigms, blueprints, structures and models of ministry). The strategy for prayer is to first pray for new wineskins so that you will have the room and the capacity to contain the new wine. New wine without a new wineskin will cause an implosion in your ministry and release mass confusion because a new move of God arrived at a time when the people were unprepared to receive it.

When new wineskins are put in place, you will then have the structure in operation that will receive and embrace present moves of God. Then when the new wine comes, it will fill you to a greater weight (in anointing, grace and ministry mantles), a greater capacity (to perform the perfect will of God) and a greater expansion (to advance the Kingdom of God) to produce a greater harvest (saved, delivered and transformed creatures).

The key to your success in ministry lies in your connection with the throne of God to get sudden and spontaneous revelation, wisdom, knowledge and prophetic strategy that will fill you to a greater capacity in order to maximize your harvest.

This is why we cannot pass out bible tracts to everyone we see on the street corner or else these tracts will simply be thrown into the trash while we are left to contemplate why we wasted the time, energy and money that was needed to print these tracts. We cannot just canvas every neighborhood we see and knock on everyone's door and expect to see harvest. Because you may be rudely ordered to get off of a person's property or have someone's guard dog chase you off of their doorstep if these people are content with their current lifestyle and mindset.

But the wisdom of God tells us which person to talk to, which time to talk to them, how to talk to them and what content to share with them.

A person could be sitting on your job right now working next to you in the same department for the first five months of their employment, but God tells you to wait and don't witness to them because it isn't time yet. But right around the sixth month, God tells you to engage them in casual conversation, not about the gospel, but about life in general. When you obey God, you will then find out that the person opens up to you immediately and confesses how they just went through a suicide attempt at the end of the fifth month and is searching for a reason to live this month. It is at this point that God will prompt you to share your life experiences and how the power of Christ has changed your life for the better after going through a similar dissatisfaction with your own life. Now had you witnessed to them at any time prior to the sixth month, their heart and mind would have been closed to you and consequently they would not have opened up to you or received your message. Not only that, but by not waiting for the right timing, it could sabotage your attempts to evangelize them at a later date simply because they have already made up in their minds that they don't want to receive anything that you have to say either now or later.

But by not rushing and instead waiting for the right prophetic timing to approach them, you will find that their pride has now been broken down on the sixth month and their heart and mind are now open to salvation. It is now that the Lord tells you to go find them in the back corner of the cafeteria break-room where you will then be successful in telling them about the Lord and how he desires them to be saved, healed and made whole. Simply telling people that they need to get saved to go to heaven in order to avoid hell is not using wisdom or strategy.

This is why in addition to the wisdom that it takes to win souls, you will also need enduring patience and love. Give them time to view the light of Christ within you that shines outwardly and also let them observe the fruit of the Spirit that manifests from within you. Let them take inventory of your fruit and be attracted to that first and then they will be further attracted to the promise of a better quality of life for themselves, once they see the life of Christ paying dividends for you.

You are not going to win people by doctrines alone or by engaging them in tiresome arguments and debates about theology.

People don't care how much you know until they know how much you care. This is why you will only win them properly to the Kingdom by the agape love of Christ. Love will draw them long before theology ever will.

Remember that the anointing is what is necessary to destroy the yokes of bondage, but it is the love of Christ that is necessary to draw souls into the Kingdom.

Love is patient and love is kind. Love is what will ultimately cause you to succeed in evangelism, not your 64,000 dollar words, earthly charisma or extrovert-like personality. After love has won them, then you can proceed to preaching the gospel to them that will save their soul. Once again, we must wash ourselves and our evangelistic blueprint of an obsolete strategy of leading our evangelism with doctrine and "denominational benefits" so that we can surrender to the successful strategy of leading our ministry with conquering love!

Prejudicial Evangelism

2 Peter 3:9 The Lord is not slack concerning his promise, as some men count slackness; but is longsuffering to us-ward, **not willing that any should perish, but that all should come to repentance**.

We must understand that God wants everyone to be saved. He wants the Jew and the Gentile, the rich and the poor, the bondman and the free to all come to repentance and salvation. With that in mind, we cannot dismiss how many churches within the Body of Christ have failed in this mandate to demonstrate to the world the need to save all souls. Many churches show preferential treatment and "compromised evangelism" tactics to rich people by simply inviting them to attend their churches, reserving them front row V.I.P seating during church services while those who have no money and no influence must wait in long lines to sit in the back of the church or in other seating places that offer poor vantage points of the church service.

The intention here is for those churches to have the rich people become members of their local church so that the rich will then contribute large tithes and offerings in the offering basket without being properly evangelized into the Kingdom of God. The rich have been handled with "kid gloves" by these churches not emphasizing the need for the rich to come to repentance and salvation. This is because they believe that the call for repentance will offend the rich and then the rich will leave and take their large tithes and offerings with them to sow their seed into a more comfortable church that won't put such demands upon them.

These churches make the unsaved rich feel accepted as if they were already saved and make them feel as if they were already a fellow brother or sister in Christ for these same fears. And as they walk on eggshells with the rich, they approach the poor with an iron clad fist. I have seen the unsaved poor treated spitefully by their own church members and talked down to in a very condescending manner. They have been treated indifferently in an unloving way as their own brothers and sisters in Christ despise them in their hearts just because they are poor. Essentially, they are treated just like they are "nobodies".

James 2:1 refers to this type of treatment as "respect of persons". Respect of persons is in reference to "partiality". In this case, the church was being partial to rich people *because* they were rich and affluent while the poor faithful saints who didn't have money, influence or affluence were being secretly despised by their own local church even though they were faithful to God and faithful to the church ministry. This is not the way of Christ, nor is it the character of Christ. When we bring worldly prejudices into our evangelism, we in essence sabotage the cause of Christ. Christ died on the cross to save all of mankind, not just the "rich" mankind.

Another example of prejudicial evangelism is racial prejudice. I have seen denominations that are predominately one race or nationality go out and aggressively evangelize lost souls that are of their own race and ethnicity, but do not have that same passion and zeal to evangelize people that come from different races, creeds or colors. This is also another example of "respect of persons" and will begin to manifest its conditional love to those races that they are prejudiced *for* while no love will come to those races that they are prejudiced *against*. Additionally, prejudicial evangelism can also manifest within a single race. If one member of a particular race has one cultural upbringing and another person of the same race has a different cultural upbringing, then the first person who becomes an evangelist may show indifference towards the second person when that first person conducts evangelistic ministry. This is an example of a person's earthly culture superseding Kingdom culture. Whenever our earthly culture influences us to compromise Kingdom culture, then that is a hallmark of idolatry. This practice and preferential treatment should never happen and is a powerful stronghold that soils many Christians' evangelism efforts as well as their worship.

Evangelism teams that operate in prejudicial evangelism will begin to take on a spirit of indifference and won't make a strong push to witness the gospel to people outside of their own race or culture and that is why they continue to hold people that are outside of their fleshly preferences at an arm's length.

They may make a general call for salvation, but they won't attempt to establish any type of relationship with you to make a *specific* call to salvation.

When relational contacts are not established, it makes the preaching of the gospel indifferent and loveless because there is no agape love present that is needed to bridge the gap between the message of the gospel and the soul that needs salvation.

But I want you to know that this is all wrong!

God does not accept prejudicial evangelism nor does He give His blessing to those evangelism teams that operate with such prejudices in their hearts.

The evangelism team must first drop everything that they are doing, sit down and then yield to the process of deliverance ministry to deliver themselves from their own prejudices before they pick up their nets to go out to evangelize again.

Any team member of an evangelism team that operates in unrepentant racial or cultural prejudice is setting themselves and the rest of their team up for ministry failure.

This was a huge stumbling-block for the Apostle Peter (a Jew) because he believed that all Gentiles were unclean. Then after the Lord showed him the vision of the four-footed beasts, creeping things and fowls of the air along with its correct meaning, Peter then had to surrender to the will of God to *renew* his mindset in order to rid himself of his former racial, national and cultural prejudices.

But before Peter could come to terms with his prejudice and subsequent deliverance, he had to first get a revelation! His enlightenment and the renewing of his mind had to first take place before he could understand and embrace the fact that the Gentiles were also offered salvation as well as the Jews. This vision that Peter saw also had to occur *before* God could give him his next ministry assignment as God was sending him to the house of Cornelius to preach the gospel to a group of Italians. Because when we start thinking that our race and our culture is better than others, we will begin to start thinking that only our race, our nation and our culture deserves to be saved more than others. In this way, we can develop what I like to call a strong sense of "racial entitlement" where we believe that our race receives salvation first while other races are either undeserving of salvation or have to wait their turn in line behind us to receive salvation. This is a no-no.

This is why in the process of us washing our nets, there is a strong element of deliverance that takes place as we purge ourselves of our old ways of thinking to then be renewed in the spirit of our minds. This is necessary to have the ability to transact Kingdom business with the right heart, the right mind and the right spirit.

All peoples and nations can't see the light of Christ within you if you are only showing that light to one race.

As Matthew 5:14 indicates, we are the light of the world, not the light of the part of the world that we are only comfortable with! So therefore, this is not a gospel to whites only, blacks only, or to Hispanics or Asians only, but it is for every man and woman on the face of this earth. How can you say that you are taking the gospel to the nations when your heart is prejudiced *against* the nations?

Uprooting Proselytization

Matthew 23:15 <u>Woe to you, scribes and Pharisees, hypocrites! for you compass sea and land to make one proselyte, and when he is made, you make him two-fold more the child of hell than yourselves</u>.

Proselytization is a common practice among many churches that is aimed at recruiting (and not evangelizing) people into church membership and enrollment into seminary institutions with the intention of making them religious proselytes. Simultaneously, these same churches shirk their responsibilities of conducting true evangelism and Kingdom discipleship.

The word "proselyte" comes from the Greek word "proselutos" which means "convert". This system of recruitment is not a conversion into the Kingdom of God. But rather, it is a conversion into religious and pagan systems as well as old moves of God that are now obsolete. A proselyte originally referred to a Gentile person that left their Gentile religion in order to convert to Judaism. In order for these people to be accepted into Judaism, they had to be naturally circumcised and then keep the Torah (law of Moses). Natural circumcision in males involved the cutting of the foreskin of a man's genitalia while in females it is the removal of the clitoris from the female genitalia or the repositioning of the labia within the genitalia. Today's modern definition of a proselyte has been expanded to include any person that converts to any religious faith or sect.

Today's application of proselytization, however, has less to do with natural circumcision and more to do with the *spiritual castration* of men and women into a system of man-made religion and tradition.

By castration, I mean that the Kingdom identity, purpose and destiny of a person have been aborted due to that person's immersion into a false, pagan system and culture of error and ignorance. When a man or woman's spiritual ability to birth purpose, reproduce the plans and purposes of God in the earth and procreate ministry sons and daughters to carry on these legacies into future generations has been taken away, then that man or woman cannot sow or reproduce the seed of the Kingdom.

When spiritual castration abounds, then men of God cannot move in seed reproduction or beget sons and daughters in the gospel due to their own spiritual emasculations. Simultaneously, women of God cannot conceive their vision, carry their purpose or birth Kingdom movements and the spiritual children necessary to carry on the legacies of the Kingdom. If there is no strength in a person's spiritual loins, then they cannot spiritually reproduce the DNA of God in family, ministry, business or government, nor can they rise up to pursue their godly purpose due to these demonic castrations that halt their purpose. Consequently, their ministries and their overall Kingdom impact will be weak and ineffective because of a loss of godly strength, power and Kingdom authority.

When proselytization is repeated often enough, it will abort the vehicle of discipleship and the harvest of son-ship in the saints. It will also abort the birthing and the raising up of a generation of godly men and women that will give God glory.

Discipleship processes the people of God into sons of God, but if proselytization were ever to prevail across the earth, then Kingdom son-ship would be aborted. In this way, proselytization sabotages evangelism by substituting religious recruitment for repentance and then castrates discipleship by aborting son-ship before the sons of God are even birthed into manifestation. This is why, to this present day, the earnest expectation of the "creature" (creation) is *still* waiting for the manifestation of the sons of God (Romans 8:19)! How long will the disobedience of mankind make the creature wait before the earth can yield her harvest?

The spirit of religion (that impersonates the Spirit of Christ) works through many churches across the globe to aggressively recruit people into a demonic system of spiritual enslavement in order to prevent them from entering into the Kingdom of God to walk the course of dominion.

Proselytization is a poor substitute for evangelism and discipleship and must be uprooted. As mentioned, proselytes are merely recruits and converts that readily assimilate themselves into religious systems without going through any actual repentance unto salvation that comes through a genuine Kingdom conversion.

Disciples of Christ, however, are actual learners and followers of Christ. So whenever a Christian ministry's mandate is to aggressively recruit people into their church for the express purpose of converting them into religious proselytes, racial and ethnic proselytes, cultural proselytes or national proselytes, then the entire operation of their ministry has essentially stopped working in their Kingdom mandate of evangelism and discipleship to instead pursue an idol.

This is that anti-Christ spirit that works in conjunction with the spirit of Molech (a demonic territorial principality) to cause underdevelopment in the saints in order to keep them at the milk levels of the word of God and remedial levels of Christianity so that they cannot progress into higher realms of eating stronger meat to become perfected sons of God.

Church members could be sitting up in the church house for thirty and forty years and never come to any level of maturity or a complete understanding of their identity or purpose in Christ. They are still in the early stages of underdevelopment in their Christian walk due to their church not being a house of deliverance, empowerment, growth or progression.

The demonic spirit of Molech specializes in the spiritual abortion of people's God-ordained destinies.

One of the greatest operations of this spirit and the anti-Christ spirit moving in many religious churches is to prevent their recruits, converts, church members and seminary students from entering into the Kingdom of

God to become disciples of Christ. Their definition of "conversion" is really assimilation into a system of religion while we understand that true discipleship is a true conversion into the Kingdom and then progression within the Kingdom. But these churches that partake in such evil deeds and practices of spiritual castration have forfeited their entire mandate given to them by the Great Commission and sabotaged their entire evangelism due to the demonic influences, pollutions and corruptions of the world.

Therefore, these local churches cannot penetrate the cultures of society to convert regions and territories because their ministries have not produced disciples of Christ that have the ability to walk in Kingdom son-ship.

If saints never become sons of God, then they can never take dominion in the earth.

But the Great Commission tells us to teach and to baptize all nations (Matthew 28:19). The spirit of religion will castrate you, but the Spirit of Christ will circumcise you (in the heart and the spirit).

Churches must disannul their generational covenants with masquerading and impersonating demons and let strong deliverance ministry and breakthrough go forth in their assemblies in order to uproot religion's fruit of proselytization.

When generational covenants with demons are finally broken, then the corresponding generational curses of those covenants will also be broken.

When is the Church going to stop recruiting proselytes and return to her original dominion mandate to teach, baptize and make disciples of all nations who are obedient to the faith to spread the gospel of the Kingdom world-wide? We need to wash ourselves and our nets of any and all spiritual perversions that can taint our evangelism so that we can properly execute our Kingdom mandates in integrity, honor and power. Our ministries must produce dominion chasers!

Deliverance From The Spirit Of The World

Romans 12:2 And don't be conformed to this world: but be transformed by the renewing of your mind, that you may prove what is that good, and acceptable, and perfect will of God.

The evangelist, evangelism team, any Christian and the Body of Christ corporately must not be conformed to this world. When we look at the word "conformed", it is in reference to "acting in accord with the prevailing standards, attitudes and practices of society". Another definition is "to become similar in form, nature or character".

A truism that is often overlooked by many local churches when forming their evangelism teams is that before they can take the gospel into the world, they must first gain complete deliverance from the spirit of the world.

After all, how can you show that you are the light of the world if you are always lighting your candle and setting it under a bush? The bible tells us not to love the spirit of the world and that whosoever shall be a friend of the world shall be the enemy of God. Again Jesus tells us that we are in the world, but we are not of the world. So if you find that you are still ensnared by a worldly mindset, thought process, way of thinking or spirit, then you are not going to be an effective Kingdom evangelist until the day you get deliverance from the snares of the world.

A senior leader who knowingly sends out the evangelist or evangelism team that is weak in the faith and that has not been delivered from the spirit of the world will ultimately set them up for ministry failure.

The senior leader, by their presumptuousness, negligence and premature sending of evangelists, can unknowingly steer them towards apostasy because they are still novices in the faith. These novices will be immature in their handling of the ministry and the Word of God and consequently will come to despise their stewardship in shameful dishonor because of gross immaturity. Before the evangelist can truly become effective in preaching the gospel to the world, they must first gain deliverance from the world. Worldly mindsets, cultural strongholds, pagan rituals, compromised belief systems and ungodly character will always sabotage your evangelism and its potential harvest.

Non-deliverance and agreement with the spirit of the world will produce a harvest of apostate evangelists ready for re-assimilation back into the world's system of religion and tradition that is void of godly power, authority and purpose.

The best that apostate evangelists can do or ever hope for is to *merge* with the culture of worldly society because they have the same spirit of the culture that they "think" they are penetrating. And you cannot deliver people from the spirit of the world if you carry that same spirit because the sword and the arrow that you use to pierce and penetrate the world cannot achieve their objectives because they have blunt edges.

The only way an evangelist can effectively penetrate the cultures and systems of worldly society is to gain complete and total separation from the spirit of the world so that there is no spiritual agreement with the system of the world.

Then they will be free of any and all stumbling blocks and snares when they go back into the world to preach the gospel of the Kingdom to save many souls. If an evangelist hasn't undergone the necessary requisite deliverance from all the trappings and snares of the world, then they have no business sowing Kingdom seed into the world or becoming part of any evangelism team until the day they drop their preaching schedules, postpone their travel itineraries and cancel their radio and TV engagements to then sit down and get some deliverance.

How can you sow good seed into the world when the seed has been corrupted due to the sower's conformity with the world? And how can you be a true light of the world if your life and ministry are always merging with the darkness of the world? So then the evangelist who truly wants to be a "fisher of men" has to break their agreement with the spirit and system of the world so that their fishing reels can be properly baited to reel in the right catch.

So to summarize, an evangelist that has not gained the necessary deliverance from the world, but still has a worldly mindset and belief system, can never hope to penetrate the culture of society with the gospel because the evangelist and the world both have the same spirit and are therefore in spiritual agreement.

All they can hope to do at this point is to merge or assimilate with the culture of society rather than penetrate it. This means that the world will succeed in pulling the evangelist into a state of apostasy and compromise where they are no longer living for Christ because they never escaped the spiritual snares, entanglements and trappings of the world. This is why experiencing salvation alone is not good enough for any person or people wanting to get involved with evangelism. They must also go through the process of progressive deliverance through discipleship to be transformed by the renewing of their minds in order to properly please God and perform His perfect will.

Man is a trilogy: body, soul and spirit. Therefore, a crucial part of a person's progression in Christ is when they gain progressive deliverance in their *inner* man.

The inner man is comprised of the soul (mind, will, intellect and emotions) and the spirit. The soul is composed of the mind, the will, the intellect and the emotions while the spirit of a man is comprised of the spiritual DNA and identity of a man that communes with God.

The spirit of a man is used to communicate with God in order to establish a relationship with Him whereas the components of the soul shape a man's thought process, belief systems, conversation and corresponding way of life.

Satan's entire seduction process goes through tempting a man through the gate of the soulish realm to evoke sensual desires and its subsequent compromise.

Satan's strategy is also to pollute the mind, perverting a person's way of thinking to commit unrighteous acts that will cause breaches and wounds in a person's spirit. These demonic attacks are strategic attacks aimed at sabotaging a person's ministry of evangelism (as well as other ministries) because the evangelist is still wounded by past rejections, hurts and traumas. Any evangelist who doesn't succeed in "washing" their minds of the evils of the world's influence and their past worldly experiences will easily become entangled and exploited when they go back into the world to preach the gospel. This is why the Apostle Paul says in 1 Thessalonians 5:23 that he prays that all 3 realms of a man (body, soul and spirit) are *sanctified wholly* and preserved blameless until the Lord returns for His Church.

Preaching The Right Gospel

Galatians 1:6 I marvel that you are so soon removed from him that called you into the grace of Christ to **another gospel**:

Galatians 1:7 Which is not another; but there are some that trouble you, and would pervert the gospel of Christ.

Galatians 1:8 But though we, or an angel from heaven, preach any other gospel to you than that which we have preached to you, **let him be accursed**.

Galatians 1:9 As we said before, so say I now again, **If any man preach any other gospel to you than that which you have accepted, let him be accursed**.

Remember that preaching is a tool to draw the lost to Christ while teaching is a tool to cause one to increase in the wisdom, knowledge, understanding and learning of Christ.

An evangelist's main assignment is to preach the gospel of the Kingdom. If the evangelist moves their ministry and outreach off of this foundation to preach another gospel, then they have greatly erred in their evangelical assignment. Satan will seduce people into believing that there is flexibility in what gospel you can preach because the flesh likes options. Satan will have you believing that there are many roads and many doors that lead to heaven.

He will further lead you to believe that people will still be saved off of the preaching of another "tailor-made" gospel. The evangelist, however, must guard their minds from "gospel trading" or compromising the integrity of the gospel of the Kingdom because they carry a "life-changing" and "soul-translating" message that will translate a person from the kingdom of Satan into the Kingdom of God. Satan knows this and that is why he fights hard to prevent a person from gaining entrance into the Kingdom of God because once they gain entrance, then he no longer has any power or control over them.

Once a person is under the dominion of God, Satan can no longer manipulate and control them so long as that person continues to yield to the Holy Spirit for the direction of their lives.

The gospel of the Kingdom is also known in scripture as "the gospel of the grace of God", "the gospel of Christ" and "the gospel of God". All these names refer to the *same* gospel. An evangelist must understand this and then guard themselves from the spirit of error because once seduced by a spirit of error, it will then cause them to preach "another" gospel than the one that they received from the Word of God. The devil's tactic is to divide and conquer you as well as your ministry by having you believe that these names all refer to separate gospels.

I was speaking with a gentleman a few years ago that said that the Apostle Peter and the Apostle Paul preached two separate gospels based on his interpretation of Galatians 2:7.

Galatians 2:7 On the contrary, when they saw that the gospel of the uncircumcision was committed to me, as the gospel of the circumcision was committed to Peter;

So then the gentlemen that I spoke with is in Christian ministry and is an overseer and senior leader of an entire congregation, but I understood very quickly that he was seduced and overtaken by a spirit of error. A spirit of error comes to corrupt your mind from the simplicity that is in Christ and then complicates matters further by promoting confusing theology to the masses through a confusing gospel. Most of the time, spirits of error like to hide behind religious masks, Kingdom terminologies, impressive vernaculars, religious clichés, traditions and local church protocols. These confusing gospels are intended to corrupt minds. These spirits of error will have these corrupted minds preach doctrines of error, but still have those people convinced and deluded into believing that they are preaching deep, profound things from the word of God.

A person that is controlled by a spirit of error will not be able to properly interpret scripture because they will always misunderstand the context of the scripture in question, but still convince themselves that their rigid mindset of error is the truth.

This spirit of error gives twisted and warped interpretations of scripture that releases confusion (and not peace and liberty) to get a person to walk along a different path that God has not intended. A spirit of error lacks the knowledge and wisdom of God. A spirit of error also cannot properly preach the gospel of the Kingdom for this same reason because the person in question is preaching the gospel by the wrong spirit.

Remember that a person cannot properly preach the gospel to the world unless they are first sent by God. So then Galatians 2:7 is not speaking of Paul preaching one gospel to the unsaved Gentiles and Peter preaching a different gospel with a different salvation message to the unsaved Jews. It is speaking of Paul preaching the gospel to the unsaved Gentiles and Peter preaching the same exact gospel to the unsaved Jews.

So in essence, the same gospel is being preached to two different people groups that are unsaved with the intention of saving them all.

This is why evangelists must renew their mindsets in order to keep the gospel simple and not complicated. Saving the lost is not a complicated concept. The redemption of man is within easy reach.

The power of the gospel lies in its simplicity, not its complexity.

Where we get off track is to try to be "deep" and use large, gargantuan vernaculars to show off our amazing vocabularies in order to impress people instead of keeping it simple in order to please God. And this is what the spirit of error does. It has us preach the wrong gospel and the wrong things that won't save the soul of a man or edify the spirit of a man, but will feed the flesh of a man. Simultaneously, it will deceive us into believing that we actually accomplished something significant in ministry by this deception. Therefore evangelists must keep themselves entirely free from the spirit of error!

MENDING THE NET

KINGDOM MENDING

As we enter this section of Mending The Net, we must understand that fishermen regularly and constantly mend their nets for hours at a time in order to get their nets ready for the next time that they go out to fish. Mending can be tedious, but ultimately necessary in order to ensure that fishermen's nets don't break when they go out to fish again. When we look at the word "mend", it means "to repair" or "to remove or correct defects and errors" within the net. Another definition is "to put in order, equip, arrange or adjust".

In the context of fishermen mending their nets, it is to prepare and perfect the net in order to get it ready for the next catch. A lot of times, mending nets can be time-consuming because you have to analyze every detail of the net to make sure that there are no weak links in the netting and that the net is wide enough to encompass the entire volume of the catch. Mending the net also entails that you make sure there are no loose threads in the netting so that the net is strong enough for reuse. Sometimes in the process of mending the net, you are actually making it stronger and better than it was the last time you went fishing in order to haul in a greater harvest.

The Point of Intersection

When fishermen mend their nets, their attention to detail is very meticulous. As we understand this, we must also understand that as they examine the threading of the net, they make doubly sure that each horizontal line of threading properly intersects with each vertical line of threading so that the net has balanced strength. The net must have balanced strength in the entire framework of netting so that it can properly balance and support the entire weight of the catch. If there is any loose or frayed threading, then that particular section of the net is potentially weak. The strongest place of netting in the entire framework is always found at the points of vertical and horizontal intersection.

The strongest point of intersection in any evangelism ministry is when that ministry intersects with lost souls when they are at a crossroads in their lives and are hungry for a better quality of life.

This is what is known as **gospel intersection**. It is the act of heaven coming down in a vertical descent and direction to intersect with a person's life and their horizontal walk on this earth to change it for the better. When the 2nd Adam (Jesus Christ) came down from heaven to intersect His Kingdom with the offspring and descendants of the 1st Adam (mankind) on earth, Jesus was able to form Himself a Bride. When the Holy Ghost came down from heaven and intersected with the apostles in the upper room on the Day of Pentecost, the results were explosive! So the principle is that whenever heaven and earth come together to meet at a critical point of intersection, the results are always miraculous and life-changing!

Every evangelism team must properly mend their strategies on how to *position* the gospel in such a way that it will *intersect* with a person's life. This means that the message of the gospel intersects with a person right where they are in life and right at the path that they are currently walking in order to draw them to repentance that will result in their salvation. When we intersect a person's life with the gospel, we are essentially finding them on the path that they are currently walking and then presenting the better path to travel so that they can reverse their course to reach their destination of godly purpose.

People may have emotional wounds and regrets about their lives and are contemplating suicide because their hope is dwindling, but as soon as the gospel intersects with them right when they are at the *crossroads* of hopelessness in their life, they will then respond appropriately to embrace the gospel's salvation message to transform their lives.

They may also be at a time in their life where they have lingering voids in their souls and nothing that they try to do in their own strength can medicate, soothe or remove those voids of debt, discontent, distress and dissatisfaction with their lives. But when the gospel intersects with them right at their voids of lack to bring in strong solutions of abundance, they will allow the word of God to fill their voids by becoming engrafted into a Kingdom that can and will answer all of their needs.

The key to all of this is proper positioning. And the key to proper positioning requires wisdom and strategy. The evangelist must have the wisdom and the strategy to meet a person right where they are on their journey in life and then properly intersect that life with the good news of the gospel. This is why we cannot wait for people to come out to our churches and sign membership forms to become members of our local church. We must go out into the world to get them!

This is how agape love is better demonstrated to the world because we go to them instead of requiring them to come to us.

Remember that God so loved the world that He gave His only begotten Son that whosoever believes on Him should not perish, but shall have everlasting life. The Father sent the Son into the world to sacrifice Him so that the world could have access to the Father through the vehicle of the Son. The Son of God is the point of intersection for divinity and humanity and is also the point of intersection where divinity *encounters* humanity. He was fully man and fully God. Heaven is God's throne and the earth is His footstool. Man's jurisdiction of dominion is in the earth. The cross (vertical and horizontal crossbars) of Christ was the infallible vehicle that granted mankind divine access and reconciliation back to God because it elevated Jesus to hang in a vertical position between both realms of heaven and earth and then released His sinless blood to over mankind. Jesus Christ was able to bridge heaven and earth together through the powerful vehicle of the cross!

Additionally, the body of Jesus was positioned on the cross in such a way that His head rested right at the points of vertical and horizontal intersection. So when God's *headship* can rest with humanity, then His government and His Kingdom can firmly be established in the earth realm. The cross was the point of intersection that enabled Jesus Christ to become the one mediator between man and God. In God's infinite wisdom, He mandated that the Son of God should be the point of intersection between God and man so that man could access grace and reconciliation through the blood of His cross. This is how Christ could be touched by the feeling of our infirmities and tempted in all points like we are and still be without sin because He was fully God and also fully man.

Jesus Christ is the point of intersection for humanity to reverse its original course towards hell to then travel its divine course towards heaven.

This is why the word of God says that God was in Christ reconciling the world to Himself because the blood of Jesus Christ became our redemption vehicle to reconcile us back into right standing with God just at the critical point of intersection in our lives.

I remember that my point of gospel intersection came back in 1991 when I was at a very low point in my life. After going through a five year depression and contemplating suicide, I was witnessed to by some people who lived in my dormitory building up at Michigan State University in East Lansing, Michigan where I was a freshman in college. What's interesting to note is that even in my depression, I didn't try to drown my sorrows by drinking alcohol or using drugs like a lot of depressed people commonly do. I didn't even have the courage to take a razor blade to slice my wrists or put a pistol to my head to pull the trigger. I was too scared to do any harm to my own body.

So I just sat there and wallowed in my own fear, apathy, heaviness and depression void of identity and direction while simultaneously losing hope quickly. It is into this bleak picture that some Christians came into my life and witnessed to me the glorious message of the gospel. At first they were a little patient with me, but then their patience ran out when I didn't immediately believe the gospel. At first I didn't believe the gospel because I was proud and stubborn and felt that if I could just get some money in my pocket, a girlfriend and some other friends then things would be alright. I was using my own wisdom and trying to get myself out of a hole using my own strength. So it took me a couple of months of trying and failing in even that, but after those couple of months, I went through the worst depression of my entire life.

The Christians had already turned away from me and my dorm counselor and the on-campus psychologist she referred me to could not help me either. I was completely alone with no friends in a part of the country that I've never lived in before. It is here that God drew me to repentance on a Saturday night. Now bear in mind that this is a Saturday night that I was in my dorm room when everyone was out partying, drinking, clubbing, fornicating, getting high on drugs and having a good time. But this Saturday night was the night that I surrendered my will to God's will. I had repented of my way of doing things. So I called up one of the Christians that had previously witnessed to me and asked him for a ride to church the next day. He agreed and so the following day, we went to church.

While listening to the preacher's message, I had already made up in my mind that I wanted a better life. So at the altar call, I went up to get saved. I had already been water baptized in Jesus name a couple of months earlier, but now I needed the baptism of the Holy Ghost. So then the ministers of the church began to lay hands on me and pray for me that I would get the baptism of the Holy Ghost. I began to praise and thank God and so I kept saying, "Thank you Jesus! Thank you Jesus!" Lo and behold, after 10 minutes of repeating this, my praises got faster and faster and then it felt like I blacked out. Then when I came to again, I heard distinctly that I was speaking in a language that I had never heard before nor was I ever taught it. The powerful thing about this is that I was shouting in tongues loud and clear and also speaking the tongues fluently. It was so powerful that I could not stop speaking in tongues for a very long time.

After this, I came to realize that I was now saved! The entire church began to greatly rejoice. The gospel had met me right at my critical point of intersection! From that point on, I began to live for Christ with a new focus and a new determination to live life how it should be lived: in Christ. So then in hindsight, I realize that the gospel intersected my life right at my greatest time of need. I truly believe if I had not gotten saved when I did, then later on I might have very well mustered up the courage to commit suicide. But I thank God for my initial cowardice and subsequent reversal of my mindset to the saving of my soul. I had a destiny to fulfill!

So part of the process of mending our nets require us to get the necessary wisdom and strategy from heaven on how to properly position the gospel so that it changes people's lives. When we properly intersect people's lives with the gospel, then those lives will also intersect with Kingdom identity, purpose and destiny!

The Kingdom Call To Purpose

Matthew 4:21 And going on from that place, he saw another two brothers, James the son of Zebedee, and John his brother, in a ship with Zebedee their father, **mending their nets; and he called them**.

Matthew 4:22 And they immediately left the ship and their father, and followed him.

What is powerful about this verse of scripture is that as soon as James and John heard the voice of Jesus calling them to a purpose that was higher than what they were currently doing, they immediately forsook their old ways and thought processes of doing things in order to embrace a greater purpose for their gift to be magnified through the lens of grace.

This indicates to us that once we hear the Kingdom call in our lives to come up higher, we must immediately leave the status quo of the norm and the ritual and routine of catching natural fish in order to embrace our Kingdom purpose of becoming fishers of men.

It is only after we hear the voice of God to respond to our Kingdom call of embracing our godly purpose that we will have real contentment, peace and joy in our lives. Because once we start moving in our purpose, we will come to the understanding that we are serving a cause that is greater than ourselves. When John and

James left their father, they were in fact, leaving their comfort zones to go higher in God by pursuing their purpose.

So then the principle is that in order for us to go higher in God to pursue our godly purpose, we must renounce our religious comfort zones to experience the discomfort of an unorthodox walk and an uncommon way of life.

Furthermore, we must remain in that walk steadfastly if we are ever going to hold fast to the profession of our faith without wavering. In order to press towards the mark for the prize of the high calling of God in Christ Jesus, you must walk by faith and not by sight. So by James and John leaving their father to walk with Jesus, they were, in fact, leaving the former security of their father to embrace the greater security of God as they walked by faith. When an image is placed into a lens, the image then becomes magnified (or larger in appearance). This is what is necessary to walk with God and this is what is necessary to maximize your potential in Christ because your potential cannot be maximized until it becomes focused through the lens of your purpose.

So then purpose is the magnifier of our potential and grace is the incubator of our purpose.

The Net Menders

As we look at the formation of strong evangelism teams, we must understand that in any evangelism team you must have clearly defined mandates and separation of duties.

Peter and Andrew were the net casters while James and John were the net menders.

While many teams may only focus on casting the net, they fail to understand that the net cannot be properly cast until the net is first properly mended.

Mending the net is indicative of the tailoring, tweaking, repairing and revision of your evangelistic strategy that you will be employing to "catch" your target group.

James and John were indicative of the team's "think-tanks" that were wholly devoted to creating, revising and perfecting evangelistic strategy. James and John were devoted to mending the net (strategy) while Peter and Andrew were devoted to casting the net (preaching). So in the formation of a strong evangelism team, we must embrace the principle of two being better than one. And by implementing this biblical principle, **two team members are devoted to one area of evangelism while the other two team members are devoted to another area of evangelistic emphasis.**

Mending By Revelation

So when two devote themselves to creating the outreach strategy that is necessary to succeed in evangelism, they must first gain prophetic wisdom and revelation from the throne of God before they can attempt to create or revise evangelistic strategy. Because if you don't hear from God, you will not know how to properly mend your nets in order to catch the entire volume of the future harvest.

When Jesus found Simon, Andrew, James and John, they were already working in a natural capacity that was parallel to their Kingdom calling. As fishermen, they were skilled in catching fish. But when you hear and yield to the voice of God to accept a Kingdom call to come up higher, you will seamlessly transition from your natural profession of catching fish into your Kingdom profession of catching souls.

Mending your net by revelation is a critical part of your preparation to haul in your largest catches.

As we revise our strategies in prophetic wisdom, our strategies will become more flexible and expandable to adjust to the new target group of people that you are getting ready to preach the gospel to. As we get patterns and blueprints for evangelistic expansion, we must trust the heavenly pattern and execute this strategy in faith so that it will produce the specific harvest for which the pattern was created for. If we don't trust the pattern, then we will revert back to our own wisdom in conducting evangelistic strategy which will yield no Kingdom harvest.

Evangelistic Specialization

Simon and Andrew specialized in casting the net while James and John's expertise lay in mending the nets. Again when we reference mending the net, means to "repair the net" as well as "join the net perfectly together". This takes skill, wisdom and the prophetic instruction of the Lord so that you can strengthen the net to be strong enough and elastic enough to expand its capacity to house the *entire* volume of the catch.

Sometimes we may have a great vision and a great zeal to win many souls to the Kingdom of God, but our strategy may be too small, too rigid and too inflexible to encompass our entire vision.

So here Jesus strategically calls four different men that all work together in the same trade or industry, but had different, diverse areas of expertise that they excelled in within that industry. Within the ministry of evangelism, you may have different and diverse areas of strategic emphasis. It's the same company, just different departments. In this way, evangelism teams must be cross-functional in nature so that they can hit multiple targets on their blueprint and gain greater operational efficiency through greater production, so that they can excel to a greater dynamic in their ministry of evangelism.

So then mending the net is symbolic of creating the strategy that has the right amount of space and flexible capacity that is necessary to catch the *totality* of the future harvest.

If you are an evangelist that is called and sent by God, then that means you will now have the grace to draw and win souls to Christ. So if you have four members of an evangelism team that were to combine their diverse evangelistic efforts into a single cohesive unit to execute the vision of the ministry, then the prophetic synergy and syncopation that will come from this would result in their evangelism instantly taking off and hitting a strong place of acceleration in the region that God has sent them to prosper. This is why when senior leaders build evangelism and outreach teams in the local church, they should have at least four core people on the team with two of those people specializing in a different area of emphasis.

Two should specialize in mending the net and two should specialize in casting the net.

As another strongly recommended option, two more team members should join the team to serve in the capacity of helps ministry to assist the four core members with miscellaneous needs. These miscellaneous needs include (but are not limited to): printing bible tracts, leaflets, flyers, gathering food and supplies for the team, praying for the team, emailing or direct mailing ministry flyers, ministry announcements and other administrative work. This will alleviate the other four core members of having to tend to these miscellaneous burdens so that they can stay fresh in order to devote themselves fully to their area of expertise and specialization.

This is a better strategy than everyone working on the same area of emphasis because it provides a more balanced and diversified approach to soul-winning as well as a more balanced workload for each team member.

If you have all four team members' skill-sets specializing and working in the same area of emphasis, then your team is going to clash and bump heads in the decision making process, which will disrupt team unity and ultimately sabotage the team's ministerial effectiveness to reach and save the lost.

Marketing Campaigns

I believe that every evangelism team that is aimed at reeling and hauling in large catches needs to have an aggressive marketing campaign. In their downtime, the team can develop a marketing plan to better structure and organize their evangelistic efforts with a singular focus and vision. Once each team member can see in their blueprint the demographics and psychographics of their target market, they can better understand people groups and their corresponding traits and habits.

Armed with this knowledge, the evangelism team can then come to a better understanding of their target market's mentality, mindset and culture, including their habits, their routines and how to best position the gospel at where it will *intersect* perfectly with people's lives and their normal daily routines.

The days of going into the town square, standing on top of a box and crying "Hear ye, hear ye!" are over. With several technological advancements over the last few decades, you must now devote a large portion of your advertisements and marketing efforts to publish your ministry over the Internet. That way, your ministry will have a longer reach. It will reach longer, wider and farther in a much quicker amount of time then you could possibly do by physically visiting these locations. This is why your ministry should have an official website that will itemize to the public what your intentions are and how salvation can benefit them.

Picture files can also be places on your website to give the viewer a pictorial representation of the message that you are trying to convey to them. Sometimes people need visuals to gain a better understanding of what Christ has done for them (although visual images of the person of Christ and how you think He should look should be discouraged to avoid idolatry).

But the key is to not overdue it on the visuals because that will take away from the principle of hearing the word of faith.

For that reason, audio recordings of you preaching the gospel should also be placed on the website. You never know how much impact it will have and how much work it is doing for a person's ministry. While you may be sleeping in your bed at night on one side of the world, someone on the other side of the world may be wide awake during the daytime listening to the message on your website and becoming convicted about their ungodly lifestyle to come to the place of repentance.

Furthermore, I believe that newsletters, publications, articles, journals, Internet blogs and discussion threads on social media can and should be published to the global community through online networking. You can market your ministry to the entire world simply by signing up for a Facebook account, creating a ministry page on Facebook and then start publishing the gospel from that ministry page to the entire online global community. From there, you can also join different social media discussion groups on Facebook that have different areas of specific emphasis so that you can talk about certain topics in greater detail. That way, your evangelism team can begin to market the gospel worldwide from the comfort of their homes and offices to reach a worldwide market in a shorter amount of time.

Marketplace Distribution

A great part of being able to efficiently cast your nets into the entire world is to first access the mountain of media.

You will need to implement great prophetic strategy in the mending stage to successfully accomplish effective marketplace distribution at the casting stage.

With 21st century technology at your disposal, you will be able to market the gospel to your target audience in a greater, faster and more efficient way than it has ever been done before.

As evangelism teams begin to be deployed into the marketplace, the team must consider the strategy that will be effective at penetrating existing markets and also have the prophetic foresight to anticipate and set up strategy to penetrate potential future markets that have not yet been tapped.

This will pay great dividends because it will ultimately draw consumers and business professionals to "buy" your product, which is the gospel (Isaiah 55:1). This means that not only has your target market been clearly defined, identified and located, but your method of distribution that has been given to you prophetically by the Holy Spirit has also been selected for market insertion.

This is why when we write books on evangelism, we can't just talk about what it takes for a person to get saved (although that is included). Nor can we write books on prayer that just teach us how to pray or prophetic books that only teach us how to prophesy. But there has a point to us prophesying and a point to us praying and a point to us evangelizing. **These books cannot teach us how to perfect our gift just to showcase our gift.** Jesus didn't go around town healing people, raising the dead and casting out demons just to show off his power. Those motives would have yielded no Kingdom purpose. So then there has to be a higher cause and a greater purpose for the reason that we write books and training manuals and it can't be just to collect royalties, gain fame, land TV/Radio interviews and sign up for book tours.

The greater purpose that needs to be realized, embraced and emphasized concerning our literary exploits of diverse emphasis is that we are first educating and next equipping our readers, public officials, business professionals and marketplace consumers for the purpose of taking dominion in their respective territorial spheres to occupy the land until Jesus comes back.

If taking dominion is not the focus and destination of all of our literary exploits and ministry endeavors, then we have essentially exited our godly purpose in favor of merchandising our anointing.

And with merchandising comes gift prostitution. Gift prostitution is where you exercise your gift for money, worldly fame and the praise of men. Prostituting your gift will immediately take you out of divine purpose. But we cannot prostitute our gift because we must about our Father's business!

When you go to purchase books on spiritual edification, you have to first look at the emphasis and the mandate of the book in question. A person that is interested in advancing the Kingdom of God for the purpose of taking dominion will enter into the marketplace to find and purchase books of great purpose. When they come across your book of evangelism or other books that you may have written that are of Kingdom emphasis, they may ask questions such as these:

1. How can your prayer book teach me prayer strategies on how to tear down, pluck up and root out demonic principalities in my region in order to transform prayer orientations for the purpose of maximizing my intercessions to take dominion in my territorial sphere?

2. How can your book on worship teach me to have strong sensitivity to the song of the Lord so that I can sing and play the chords of heaven to apostolically and prophetically set Kingdom atmospheres, climates and environments citywide? Furthermore, how can I use that equipping to restore a city's relationship back to God by establishing powerful, godly altars that will release pure and undefiled worship?

3. How can your book on prophecy teach me prophetic operations and how to prophesy the will of God in order for me to access open heavens so that I can gain the necessary impartation, wisdom and upgrade to release

the plans and purposes of God in the earth realm in order to properly steward a global vision?

4. How can your book on evangelism teach me effective, relevant and present day strategies on how to penetrate the cultures of society with the gospel of the Kingdom in order to save, convert, transform and translate people, people groups, creatures, cities, regions and nations from the principalities and powers of darkness into the glorious Kingdom of God?

5. How can your dominion book teach me present truth and 21st century strategies that will educate, equip and empower mankind on how to take dominion in their specific area of assignment? How can I renew my mind into a dominion-oriented mindset? And can I find your topics of dominion in multiple media formats (e-books, CD's, DVD's) for multiple vehicle distribution?

Do we have the renewed mindset necessary to have this train of thought and ask these types of questions?

These are the "dominion questions" that need to be asked as we begin to survey and peruse bookshelves and online bookstores for the right book or e-book (in addition to the Bible) that can push us into our purpose. These are also the questions that need to be raised in a person's heart when they are passionate about possessing their territory to advance the Kingdom of God. When market penetration is achieved, God will cause the gospel to flood every area of the marketplace in strong literary and other media exploits such as books, e-books, training manuals, CD's, DVD's, audio and video file formats that are all aimed at empowering those that will believe the gospel to take dominion.

When all of your business products (books, media, CD's, DVD's) become best sellers in the online marketplace, then that means that everyone is buying your products because they consider them to be better and greater than other authors' products on the same subject.

When your business competitors that have been marketing products similar to yours begin to purchase your products and adopt these products as their own standard, it means that God has made you the head and not the tail and that you are taking dominion in the marketplace.

So when God tells you to write a book and then publish that book in the marketplace, then the gospel will reach longer and farther across the earth to countries, nations and continents that you may never personally visit in your lifetime.

And when those principles that are highlighted in your books begin to penetrate and flood the physical marketplace (bookstores, newsstands, grocery stores) as well as the online marketplace, people will begin to purchase your products, learn those principles and then apply those principles to their own lives, businesses and purposes as the standard and norm of human and business culture. When people begin to embrace the principles outlined in your books to transform their own lives and businesses, then you have effectively taken dominion in the marketplace and the line and sphere of your ministry and business will extend throughout the earth to advance God's eternal Kingdom.

In essence, your literary works that have been written, published and distributed with Kingdom strategy and precision have effectively cornered the market.

Now that's dominion!

As you begin to gather book deals and your publicist schedules book tours, you can then meet people face to face to gain a strong rapport with them and also make specific relational contacts in order to jumpstart strong business relationships with them. Perhaps they can come into partnership with you to be independent distribution vehicles to initiate greater levels of expanded distribution when they market your product. When you begin to diversify and expand your distribution vehicles, then you can hit multiple areas of sphere penetration in not just the marketplace only, but also the private, public, government and nonprofit sectors of society.

Mending By Prayer

I feel that we must talk about the importance of prayer and how prayer sets the foundation for our evangelistic strategy and discourse. While in the process of mending the net, it is very important for you to retreat to your prayer room and then begin to delve deeply into prayer to gain the necessary wisdom from heaven for your evangelistic assignment. Even Jesus Christ retreated to mountains and the wilderness to pray to the Father in order to crucify the flesh and also get instructions on when and where his next preaching and teaching discourse would be. An evangelism team that does not devote themselves fully to prayer cannot get the mind of Christ on important matters nor can they receive the proper strengthening as they prepare for their next assignment.

If the team does not make prayer a priority, then they can conceivably launch an evangelism ministry (including their preaching discourses) in the flesh and then govern the direction of the ministry by their own self-will and wisdom.

Then they will deceive themselves into believing that God is telling them to conduct their ministry in this manner. This is why the team must fully devote themselves to prayer and intercession. As they set aside quality time to lay out before the Lord in prayer, intercession, meditation and study of God's Word, then God will begin to unravel the mysteries of the Kingdom to them. This will give them fresh downloads and strong upgrades so that they will be fully equipped to mend their nets with Kingdom precision in preparation for their re-entry into the world's systems in order to win more souls for Christ.

Prayer helps the evangelism team to:

1. Strengthen the spirit man in preparation to do the work of the evangelist

2. Gain sensitivity to the voice of the Lord for prophetic instructions and directions on where, when, how and which person or people group to evangelize

3. Gain access to the throne of God in order to receive fresh blueprints, spiritual impartations, witty ideas, present-day strategies and necessary upgrades that will

maximize a team's evangelism for present-day success and excellence

4. Walk in strong grace to demonstrate the Kingdom of God in all signs, wonders and miracles as they go forth to minister the gospel of the Kingdom to their God-assigned target group

5. Spend quality time with the Lord in divine communion in order to gain the mind of Christ for their lives

Romans 8:26 Likewise the Spirit also helps our infirmities: **for we don't know what we should pray for: but the Spirit itself makes intercession for us with groanings which cannot be uttered into words**.

Romans 8:27 And he that searches the hearts knows what is the mind of the Spirit, **because he makes intercession for the saints according to the will of God**.

Here the Word of God is telling us that the Holy Spirit will intercede on our behalf while we are praying in order to make intercession for us. So as we go forth into prayer, the Holy Ghost will then cause us to go into tongues and other wordless groans (sighs) that we can't accomplish in our own self-will so that our intercession can stay on the correct course and vein of prayer that runs congruent with the perfect will of God. When our prayer life begins to gain traction in the spirit realm, it will begin to access open heavens in order to gain the necessary wisdom, knowledge, revelation, understanding and strategy that will greatly enhance our evangelism to bring forth ministry success.

I truly believe that when evangelists and evangelism teams master the concepts of prayer and intercession by yielding to the Holy Spirit when they pray, then God can truly lead and guide them to which soul is ready to be evangelized. Through much time spent in prayer, God's purpose concerning their evangelism can truly be revealed to them which will upgrade their evangelistic strategy, the timing of that strategy and the method of that strategy's implementation.

Tongues of Intercession

In an earlier chapter we have established the fact that speaking in tongues is the initial sign upon receiving the baptism of the Holy Spirit. This should not be confused with the gift of tongues mentioned in 1 Corinthians 12:10. This verse of scripture reads "......to another divers kinds of tongues". The word "divers" refers to "many different kinds". So then there are many different kinds of tongues (or languages).

One day when you are praying and the Spirit makes intercession, He could cause you to go into tongues in one language and then cause you to go into another language on another day in prayer. So then we must rightly divide the word of truth in order to differentiate the tongues of Acts 2:1-4, Acts 10:44-46 and Acts 19:6 from the tongues of 1 Corinthians 12:10 and 1 Corinthians 14:2,4,13-15.

The "divers kinds of tongues" in 1 Corinthians chapters 12 and 14 is speaking of a gift of the Spirit that a person receives *after* they have already received the baptism of the Holy Spirit.

This particular gift is an utterance gift used for prayer and intercessory purposes.

When an intercessor goes into prayer, they will begin to pray in their regular language at first, but then the Holy Spirit will begin to transition their prayer into unknown tongues that the person hasn't ever learned before. As we continue to yield to speaking in tongues as God gives the utterance, we can effectively go into deeper levels of intercession and prayer.

This will result in more prayer penetrations into the heavens so that we may get a thorough impartation of wisdom, knowledge, revelation, instruction, resources, upgrades and encouragement from the throne of grace that is needed to walk out our assignment in excellence. We are using our intercession as a "spiritual drill" that will drill and plow the heavens so that we can sow Kingdom seeds into spiritual climates and atmospheres in order to yield a Kingdom harvest.

An evangelist who does not pray is an evangelist who will not have strength or strategy.

According to 1 Corinthians 14:2:

1 Corinthians 14:2 For he that speaks in an unknown tongue <u>**speaks not to men, but to God: for no man understands him; nevertheless in the spirit he speaks mysteries**</u>.

When a person goes into tongues, they will only speak to God because no one else will be able to understand them because they are speaking in mysteries. It could be the tongues of men or the tongues of angels that cannot be understood by us unless there is an interpretation. If no such interpretation exists, than that means that we are only edifying ourselves in prayer and not edifying the entire congregation.

1 Corinthians 14:4 He that speaks in an unknown tongue <u>edifies himself</u>; but he that prophesies <u>edifies the church</u>.

To edify means to "build up", "restore" or "uplift". The emphasis centers on building up, restoring or uplifting someone for the purposes of promoting their growth in Christ. When we go into prayer, we will begin to build up our spirit man through constant divine interactions and heavenly exchanges in our prayer relationship with God.

However, if there is an interpretation, then that means that God has a word for the entire local church on a corporate level and not just for you on an individual level. Tongues that are accompanied by an interpretation translate to prophecy. This could be personal prophecy (relating to just the individual in question) or it could be corporate prophecy (relating to a larger group of people). When corporate prophecy goes forth during a church service, then that means that God has a prophetic word for the entire assembly gathering. So we must understand the difference between prophecy on an individual level as opposed to prophecy on a corporate level.

1 Corinthians 14:14 For if I pray in an unknown tongue, <u>my spirit prays</u>, but my understanding is unfruitful.

Here we see the purpose of unknown tongues as it relates to intercessory prayer. The purpose for it is to help your spirit man pray to God more effectively and more fruitfully even if you don't understand what you are praying.

This can help your evangelism by strengthening your spirit man so that you feel strong, refreshed and revived to do the work of the Lord.

CASTING THE NET

KINGDOM CASTING

Casting the net refers to the actual dispensation of the preaching discourse of the gospel from its messengers to target persons, people groups and any other "creatures" in question by utilizing prophetically mended strategies that are implemented at the right time and place of God's own designation. This is done by evangelistic messengers preaching the gospel of the Kingdom that will hasten the drawing of the catch to Christ. As fishermen in the natural cast their nets into the sea to haul in large catches of fish as strong indicators and barometers of business success in their fishing trade or industry, so must evangelists cast their nets into the world to catch the souls of men into the Kingdom of God in order to indicate strong patterns and models of evangelistic success in their Kingdom business.

In essence, evangelists are fishers of men that cast the gospel into the world in order to save the souls of men.

As a fisher of men, your responsibility is to fish for men in specific places at specific times. And what helps this preaching discourse is the wisdom that is downloaded from heaven into your spirit man. Once you receive and implement this wisdom, it will ensure that your catch is first executed correctly and then after this execution is complete, the catch is then secured into a structure that has the capacity large enough to house, support and facilitate the evangelistic harvest.

Remember that in the context of a Kingdom understanding, the aim of casting the net is always focused on producing a harvest. If there is no harvest, then you have not successfully fulfilled Kingdom Casting and your evangelism will suffer greatly due to this lack of harvest and will invite God's displeasure.

Prophetic Evangelism

What is prophetic evangelism?

Prophetic evangelism is a strategic-level type of evangelism that only evangelizes individuals, people and people groups that God specifically sends you to utilizing revelatory strategy, knowledge and wisdom that comes from the throne of God to direct your evangelism efforts at specific times and places of God's designation.

The prophetic anointing in the Body of Christ points direction for which way we should walk to not only fulfill the Word of God, but also fulfill God's specific will concerning your individual course (ministry, business, family, etc.). This is the course that you need to walk in order to please God.

So then the prophetic dimension upon the ministry of evangelism acts as a director or leader, notifying us of what, when, where and how to do things that will produce evangelistic harvest.

The prophetic gives great direction to an evangelism team so that they can maximize their efforts to produce harvest in a shorter amount of time.

But not only that, the beautiful thing about this is that the prophetic allows the team to exercise great economy in their time invested and great economy in their energy expended to produce *greater* harvest in a *shorter* amount of time. This means that by yielding to the inspiration and direction of the prophetic anointing, the evangelism team can then make contact with their target groups 100% of the time to yield 100% harvest so long as they follow the leading of the Holy Spirit on how to conduct their evangelism at the time that the Holy Spirit says to move.

Without the prophetic dimension upon our evangelism, we will not receive fresh revelation on who, where and when we need to evangelize.

Consequently we will be forced to fall back on the traditionally obsolete evangelistic methods of yesteryear that won't be effective at producing today's harvest. We are living in an hour where two or more specific types of anointing must become grouped together so that we can excel in Kingdom ministry today.

Most of the time, it is the foundational dimensions of the apostolic and the prophetic anointing that must be combined with or upgrade other ministries in order to keep those ministries fresh, relevant and current so that they we can properly transact present-day dominion. This means that we must receive regular spiritual impartations and periodic and progressive upgrades in our anointing levels to keep us current with today's ministry needs for today's generational harvest.

This is why the prophetic anointing and the evangelistic anointing must undergo a marriage so that they can work together in synergy to produce a present harvest in a present generation.

The key to prophetic evangelism lies in its timing and its strategy.

When God places a prophetic dimension upon an evangelistic ministry, it is in fact an impartation of prophetic wisdom that is released upon the ministry so that the team will know how, when and where to go about their work using the revelatory strategies from heaven. The difference between producing evangelistic harvest and toiling all day and night without a single catch is the prophetic dimension.

The prophetic dimension is the common denominator that bridges the gap between your evangelism ministry efforts and your harvest.

Since the prophetic anointing is a foundational ministry in the Body of Christ, it therefore carries governmental authority. So in order for any evangelism team to flourish and have any level of success, it will require a strong impartation of the prophetic dimension and moreover, a strong implementation of a prophetic dynamic in the team's core infrastructure so that their ministry can have proper government and direction for strong levels of success. This means that personal and corporate prophecy will go forth regularly to provide godly counsel and heavenly direction to the team.

This is what we need in order to know when, where and how to cast our nets.

We need strong evangelism teams that are led and guided by the Holy Ghost in their work efforts when they go to witness the gospel of the Kingdom to the masses of humanity. Through the agency and the upgrades of the prophetic dimension, evangelism teams will begin to have a good understanding of the spiritual times and seasons as the prophetic tribe of Issachar did for Israel in the Old Testament (1 Chronicles 12:32). When evangelism teams have a good understanding of times and seasons, then they will know what to do, when to do it and how to do it. We must embrace prophetic wisdom!

Now let's look at Luke 5:1-11 to see some powerful examples of prophetic evangelism that can be extrapolated from this section of scripture.

Luke 5:1 And it came to pass, that, as the people pressed upon him to hear the word of God, he stood by the lake of Gennesaret,

Luke 5:2 And saw two ships standing by the lake: but the fishermen had left out of them, **and were washing their nets**.

So as we have learned beforehand that fishermen must wash their nets to erase the bad smell and residue of an old catch, so must we also understand that an evangelistic team has to wash away an old strategy that may have worked well in the marketplace, but won't work well in the governmental sectors of society.

Remember that nets are symbolic of the specific revelatory strategies which you must implement in your evangelism in order to properly secure your harvest of souls that are located in specific places, people groups or industries.

Luke 5:3 And he entered into one of the ships, which was Simon's, and asked him to thrust out a little from the land. And he sat down, and taught the people out of the ship.

Luke 5:4 Now when he had finished speaking, he said to Simon, **Launch out into the deep, and let down your nets for a catch**.

Here, prophetic evangelism is operating in earnest. The instruction was to:

1. Launch out into the deep

2. Let down their nets for a *promised* catch

When you wait for the prophetic instructions of the Lord to direct you to the right place to which you must cast your nets and then follow those instructions to completion, you will reap a great harvest because you have used great strategies.

The intention is to reel in or haul in the catch into a structure large enough and suitable enough to house, service and maintain the harvest.

Remember that Jesus commanded them to let down their nets (plural) which meant that He wanted them to let down more than one net.

Luke 5:5 And Simon answering said unto him, Master, we have toiled all night, and have caught nothing: **nevertheless at your word I will let down <u>the net</u>**.

Peter's mindset was in a place of limitation because he tried to fish all night long using his own strength and wisdom, but caught nothing because of the absence of divine prophetic direction. So in his frustration and exhaustion, he only partially heard the command of Jesus. Jesus told him to cast down his nets (more than one), but Peter in his fatigue and embarrassment only heard "net" and that is why he cast down only one net, which was not the Lord's command. When an evangelist only executes partial obedience, this will result in incomplete preparation and poor execution of the mandate.

This is why we have to be in the right spiritual place to hear the commands of God clearly.

That means that prayer and fasting is needed to break yokes and strongholds of spiritual deafness. If we don't clearly hear all of the entire strategies, then we can sabotage our own harvest by implementing only part of the strategy because we listened to the Lord with only half an ear. As we will see in the next verse, using only one part of the entire strategy will now sabotage their entire preparation to catch the totality of the harvest.

Luke 5:6 <u>And when they had this done, they enclosed a great multitude of fishes: and their net broke</u>.

Because Peter did not properly follow instructions in verse five to implement *all* of the strategies that the Lord had commanded and not just a single strategy, his one net did not have the elasticity, capacity or the strength necessary to handle the entire weight and volume of the total harvest.

Because when the harvest is great, we may have to spend more time implementing two or three strategies instead of just one in order to have the ability and the capacity large enough to reel in our *total* harvest.

If we only implement one strategy, then that one strategy may not have the strength to handle the entire weight of the harvest. This is why we must spend much time in the place of prayer hearing the instructions of the Lord to receive the necessary revelation on how to properly mend our nets before we cast them into the sea of men.

As we repair our evangelism strategies to perfection, we will then be fully prepared to preach the gospel of the Kingdom to the various people groups that are being controlled by the world's systems. We must hear from God *clearly* and *completely* before we begin to implement evangelistic strategy, so that after implementation, we can begin preaching our evangelistic discourse in our places of assignment with great productivity, efficiency and excellence.

Partnerships Of Purpose

Luke 5:7 And they beckoned to their partners, which were in the other ship, **that they should come and help them**. **And they came, and filled both the ships, so that they began to sink**.

In the natural, before fishermen can haul in a huge catch of fish, they must first consider the weight and the volume of the fish and then check to see if their ship can *sustain* that level of weight so that the structure of the ship can stay afloat *after* it receives the harvest. This must be factored into their strategy *before* they embark and set sail to catch their fish. Because once fishermen cast their nets into the sea to then haul in a great catch of fish out of the sea back onto their ships, their ships must have the ability to stay afloat to be able to transport the fish back to shore.

In addition, as soon as they make the catch, they must immediately transition the catch into a freezer to preserve them so that the catch doesn't spoil. This is why they cannot leave the fish tied up in the net and then leave it sitting out on the bow or stern of the ship exposed to the sun. If the fish are not immediately frozen and are instead left exposed to the sun, then their flesh will become slippery and slimy and will be very hard to cut and clean later because they have become spoiled. If the fish spoil, then they cannot be sold to the market for a profit because they will endanger food safety health standards.

Then the fish markets and other seafood restaurants, in turn, cannot sell the fish to the public for a profit for these same reasons because the market or restaurant can't cook spoiled fish and serve it to the public. The reason for this is because they have to stay in adherence to FDA (Food and Drug Administration) food safety standards of public health regulations or else they are in trouble of getting negative health ratings, having their food licenses revoked and their shops and places of business closed down. Because when a restaurant chef cooks spoiled fish, it will cause a foul odor to be smelled throughout the entire building. This is why after catching the fish, fishermen must have the skill and the wisdom on how to *maintain and preserve* the fish until the ship gets back to shore. Once they are back on land, they have to immediately transition the fish to a building that also has freezers. The fish must be kept in those freezers until fishermen are ready to cut, clean and cook the fish.

Let's look at the word "ships" from Luke 5:7.

A ship is a symbolic representation of the *physical structure* that has the capacity to house the totality of the coming harvest.

This could be a local church, a house ministry, a cell ministry or a homeless shelter that provides refuge to transients, depending on the number of souls that get saved. All of these types of housing represent ship vehicles that can house and transport the evangelistic harvest into places of spiritual maintenance, sanctification, growth and progression.

If the structure of your ministry is not large enough to handle the entire volume of your harvest, then your ministry (ship) will become overburdened by the tremendous ingathering of volume and that will render your structure insufficient due to the lack of space and manpower that's necessary to sustain it.

This will cause your ministry to start sinking into frustration, despair and ministry failure. And this type of limitation will ultimately frustrate your purpose in evangelism. With both ships and both sets of partners working together, those structures were still insufficient to stay afloat in ministry because the harvest that God had designated for them exceeded their expectations and therefore their preparation.

And whenever we get to the place where our expectation falls short of our preparation and our preparation falls short of our harvest, then we are in trouble!

If a ministry finds that their ministry structure and their capacity for housing the harvest falls far short of the expectation of their vision, it is because they didn't do a good enough job of mending their nets (assessing their strategies of how to house and support the harvest) before they started casting their nets into the sea to evangelize. Your evangelism ministry and strategy (nets) may serve as a temporary holding place for newly saved people (fishes), but your evangelism ministry cannot be a permanent place of housing and progression for saved people moving higher in God and moving further along in their purpose to reach their prophetic destiny (shore).

They will need a strong local church with a competent overseer that is able to facilitate their growth.

Babes in Christ are at a very delicate time in their lives. They don't know their own way and so they have to be guided on the right path. If they are not guided on the right path, then they are open to deception, error and manipulation if they do not immediately progress into discipleship. Therefore after salvation they need to be transitioned immediately into discipleship (another ship vehicle needed to transport them to shore) so that they do not become spiritually spoiled (fish exposed to the sun) and their future public ministries do not become sabotaged because of the corruption (more sun exposure) they may have experienced in their spiritual infancy (right after the catch). After fish are caught, they are not supposed to stay in the net. They are supposed to be placed into the freezer (house of God)!

This will require competent manpower that has the ability (grace) to transport and service the harvest. For the requisite manpower needed for this transportation, we will need to form strong Kingdom partnerships.

When you don't have the foresight to properly anticipate the level of manpower and partnerships that are needed to facilitate your harvest, then your ministry will begin to sink into stress, anxiety, frustration, heaviness and depression.

When this happens you will not be in the right frame of mind mentally, emotionally or spiritually to witness the gospel to your potential harvest. Nor will you have the sufficiently prepared manpower or on-staff personnel that can transfer the harvest into a ministry structure that has the capacity and the ability to immediately transition the harvest into strong progressive periods of discipleship.

The progression of salvation is discipleship and if our evangelism cannot successfully "hand-off" the harvest to a ministry structure that can properly disciple them into son-ship, then we will essentially drop the ball on our responsibility to lead a newly saved person into a greater place of progression and enlargement.

This is why you must have a strong helps ministry to offer you continual support as you ingather the harvest.

Two members will mend the nets, two will cast the nets and generally two others should serve as a helps ministry to support the entire team.

Without a strong helps ministry, then resources, assistance and manpower will begin to dwindle and then the other four team members will not be able to properly take up all the burdens of the ministry to set them upon their shoulders. Had Simon Peter understood this principle early on, then he, Andrew and their partners that were located in the other ship would have been working together in two larger ship structures that had the power to haul in the tremendous harvest and still stay afloat in the process. Remember that in order for the nets to work properly, all team members must be on one mind and one accord, staying in their respective lanes, working together in unity, synergy and syncopation.

Evangelism is hard work and requires a lot of time invested, manpower and attention to detail. Moses couldn't keep the rod of God lifted up over his head all day long so that Israel could win the battle. He had to have Aaron and Hur (helps ministries) to assist him in keeping the rod of God lifted in order for Israel to prevail over her enemies. The weight of the rod was too heavy to keep it lifted over his head alone. This is why ministry leaders should not try to do everything themselves. They need to start identifying their Aarons and Hurs today to form effective team ministries! This is the essence of NET-WORKING!

Luke 5:8 When Simon Peter saw it, he fell down at Jesus' knees, saying, Depart from me; for I am a sinful man, O Lord.

Luke 5:9 <u>For he was astonished and all that were with him, at the catch of the fishes which they had taken</u>:

Once again, Peter and his partners' shortsightedness in direction, preparation and expectation caught them off guard when the harvest actually came because they failed to pay attention to the prophetic. We need ministry gifts that will walk in tremendous faith, bold vision and prophetic wisdom that will constantly keep raising the bar on their level of expectation so that they can prepare to receive greater harvest!

Luke 5:10 <u>And so was James, and John, the sons of Zebedee, which were partners with Simon</u>. And Jesus said to Simon, **<u>Fear not; from this time forward, you shall catch men</u>**.

Notice here that the scripture says that James and John were *partners* with Simon. This is what is critical in the formation of a strong evangelism team.

Until you have gifted and fruitful ministers of God who work in different areas of evangelistic emphasis and function who will willingly come together into *partnership*, then you cannot be successful in your evangelism ministry.

Until you break the strongholds of limitation off of your mindset to renew your mind and expand your capacity, you will not be able to properly process or service the large ingathering of souls coming into your ministry through the powerful tool of prophetic evangelism. As we begin to tap into the powerful principles of prophetic evangelism, our ministries and business professions will begin to work together in tandem with each other to advance the Kingdom of God in our God-assigned territories and regions.

Luke 5:11 And when they had brought their ships to land, **they forsook all, and followed him**.

Once the partners began to see the results of Kingdom harvest properly modeled in the earth, they immediately abandoned their normal thought processes concerning standard business practices of fishing to allow the Kingdom model that they had just witnessed to transform their mindsets into a greater paradigm of Kingdom business. They would now be fishers of men, but they would be fishers of men for a greater purpose than just recreational fishing or fishing for a profit. When we enter into purpose, then we will begin to render our gifts, talents and anointing to serve a cause that is greater than ourselves just as soon as we embrace the mind of Christ to prosper and have good success.

The Parable of the Great Banquet

Now let us examine the parable of the Great Banquet in Luke 14:15-24 to extrapolate more principles of prophetic evangelism.

Luke 14:15 And when one of them that sat at the table with him heard these things, he said to him, Blessed is he that shall eat bread in the kingdom of God.

Luke 14:16 Then said he to him, <u>A certain man made a great supper, and invited many</u>:

Luke 14:17 And sent his servant at supper time to say to them that were invited, <u>Come; for all things are now ready</u>.

Luke 14:18 And they all with one consent began to make excuses. The first said to him, I have bought a field, and I must go see it; please excuse me.

Luke 14:19 And another said, I have bought five yoke of oxen, and I have to go to test them; please excuse me.

Luke 14:20 And another said, I have married a wife, and therefore I cannot come.

Luke 14:21 So then that servant returned, and showed his lord these things. Then the master of the house became angry and said to his servant, **Go out quickly into the streets and lanes of the city, and bring in here the poor, and the crippled, and the lame, and the blind**.

Here we see in the first few verses the progression of traditional evangelism to a more strategic-level evangelism that is more time-sensitive in nature with its emphasis centered on evangelizing specific people groups that were located in specific places at specific times. The initial call for evangelism was the general, universal call for everyone to come to Christ, but because many which heard the invitation put their own desires in front of God's call for salvation, it ultimately led them to despise the general invitation. Consequently, they were found *unworthy* to dine with Jesus in His Kingdom. Verse twenty-one begins the preparation and discourse of prophetic evangelism.

This is far more strategic than the traditional evangelism strategies normally employed to reach the masses because it usually yields little to no results.

Now consider the prophetic blueprint that the man gave his servant which highlights the "how", the "where", the "when" and the "who" of prophetic evangelism. The "what" is already known because the servant already knew that the "what" pertains to him bringing these people into his master's house to sit them at his master's table in order to dine with him at supper.

1. **Go quickly** (which indicates that this command is time-sensitive and so the evangelist must arise now and then proceed quickly to the place of God's designation at that specific time).

This is the "when" and the "how" of prophetic evangelism. By mastering what time you should go and how you should get there, you will become very proficient in critical areas of time management and time maximization. Your ministry will not be overextended and your body won't be overly exhausted because you have utilized great economy in your efforts expended. This allows you to properly execute prophetic evangelism in economy and excellence.

2. **Go into the streets and lanes of the city** (which indicates that the evangelist must go to strategic points of intersection within a city where the target demographic and designated people groups are presently located and are waiting to be evangelized).

This is the "where" of prophetic evangelism. This is crucial to the success of your evangelism to properly locate the souls that are waiting to be saved at strategic locations. The "where" prophetically shows us locations that will serve as our potential places of harvest so long as we conduct our evangelism *in* these places of harvest.

3. **Bring the poor, the crippled, the lame and the blind into God's house** (God will prophetically drop into your spirit which people groups are the target audience and then we must obey the instructions of the Lord to strategically evangelize these specific people groups in obedience to secure a specific harvest).

This is the "who" of prophetic evangelism. This is crucial to finding your target demographic and the specific people groups who will hear the gospel from your mouth on how to get saved.

We already know that the "what" of prophetic evangelism is to get souls saved.

So when the "how", "who", "where" and "when" have all been put together into a prophetic strategy that you can tangibly place into a viable evangelistic blueprint, then you will have the supernatural grace and ability to move effectively in strong prophetic evangelism.

Remember that true evangelists are not catch-and-release fishermen that catch fish and then release them back into the water as a hobby. They do not engage in sport fishing as a means of recreation or fishing for fun like false evangelists do.

True evangelists will always conduct their evangelism with sincere motives, enlarged hearts and agape love to move in great purpose to save the souls of mankind.

Jesus (the man that made the great supper) gave His servant the strategic locations of "streets" and "lanes of the city" and then also gave His servant (who operates as an evangelist) the target demographic and psychographic description of the people that he wanted evangelized.

Demographics deal with the age, income, occupation and education of the target group. Psychographics deal with the similar attitudes, values and lifestyles of a particular people group.

Jesus had His evangelist focus on the particular people groups that displayed specific characteristics. The designated people groups that the evangelist had to focus on were "the poor, the crippled, the lame and the blind". The reason for this is because God had deemed them worthy to sit and dine at His table.

So then the principle is that our evangelism must not focus on casting our pearls before the swine, but instead focuses on sowing the seed of the gospel into people's lives that display fruits worthy of repentance.

These people that God had deemed worthy were located in certain places where God had His servant cast his nets in order to haul in a *specific* harvest. These different categories of people indicate four separate people groups where each group had specific infirmities and similar dysfunctions in common.

The servant's harvest came from a target market that was located in two separate locations (streets and lanes of the city) comprised of four separate people groups rolled into one large catch. Let me repeat this again so that the imagery can sink in completely.

***One* evangelist cast his nets into *two* separate locations to haul in *four* separate people groups in only his *first* catch.**

This is powerful! The amazing thing is that the servant got all these souls saved in only his first penetration into the world system. And what is still so amazing about all of this is that this was only the servant's *first* catch. The servant still had more work to do and this was only his first evangelistic pass. Most outreach departments within many local churches would have been content with this level of production for an entire year's worth of evangelism and outreach, but God is showing us that we can accomplish this gargantuan level of production in only our first attempt if we adhere to His prophetic instructions correctly and completely. This is why when prophetic evangelism is strategically implemented from an evangelism team that is properly deployed, the team will then produce a great harvest on every catch.

Furthermore, he tells his servant to "go quickly" which indicates that the target groups in question would only be located in the streets and lanes of the city at that specific time, but may not be at those same locations at a later time.

Streets are an indicator of engaging persons in street evangelism at specific times and places, which requires *gospel intersection* (preaching the gospel so that it intersects with a person right where they are in life).

Lanes of the city refers to places of business traffic, commerce and other places of public gathering that requires *gospel convergence* (locating the strategic public platform at public places where large crowds and multitudes in a

city will come to converge upon that particular place of meeting to hear the gospel).

Lanes of the city indicate that the people groups that God has sent the evangelist to are located in the public sector and other lanes of convergence within the city. This could be shopping districts, government quarters or any other public areas where people congregate.

When prophetic evangelism is implemented in any outreach ministry, the results will yield 100% harvest so long as we obey the instructions of God. Because in His foreknowledge, God already knows which people have their ears, hearts and minds open to the gospel of the Kingdom and that is why He strategically steers His servants in the appropriate direction to locate those people who God has ordained to gain fellowship and reconciliation with Him.

At the same time, God causes His servants to maximize their evangelistic efforts to produce constant harvest.

Highways and Hedges

We have just discussed the Kingdom principles extrapolated from The Parable of the Great Banquet. Now let's look at the significance of **highways and hedges.**

Luke 14:22 And the servant said, Lord, it is done as you have commanded, **and yet there is still room**.

Luke 14:23 And the lord said to the servant, **Go out into the highways and hedges, and compel them to come in so that my house may be filled**.

Luke 14:24 For I say to you, That none of those men which were invited shall taste of my supper.

The servant's 1st catch called for him to bring in four separate people groups from two different locations. Now the 2nd catch calls for the servant to go out again to find more souls that are located in the highways and hedges. The reference to "highways" indicates that the servant will now have to travel a further distance to locate and bring more souls into his master's house then he had to do on his 1st catch.

This means that he now has to expand the scope of his search. He has to take his evangelism to the highways where he will then expand his evangelism ministry into wider areas of neighboring villages, towns and possibly other cities.

"Highways" indicates that your evangelism has to expand the scope of its search, its reach and its evangelistic focus to sow the seed of the gospel in a wider arc in order to reach many more people over a larger region of territory.

"Hedges" refers to people that are located in places that are not immediately visible to the natural eye. When God sends you to the hedges, He is sending you to evangelize people that dwell in isolated and hidden places.

Sometimes people dwell in isolated, out of the way places such as the desert, the wilderness, forests, mountain ranges and other places that are not within easy reach. The people that live in these places need salvation, but are currently living in places of isolation and solitude.

So while the streets and lanes of the city are representative of prophetic evangelism, highways and hedges are representative of apostolic evangelism (which we will learn later on).

Prophetic evangelism is the catalyst for harvest and apostolic evangelism is the progression of harvest.

Evangelism's 1st mandate is prophetic in its orientation and then its 2nd mandate is apostolic in its momentum. Foundational evangelism to the streets and lanes of the city gains the necessary traction to set the stage for a new dynamic that will build the momentum of progressive evangelism to the highways and hedges. This is how evangelism starts strategically from a specific point of origin and then fans outward and onward by building momentum.

So then the principle is that we cannot move effectively in the momentum of apostolic evangelism unless we first master the foundational principles of prophetic evangelism.

Verses 23 and 24 of Luke chapter 14 also tell us that general invitations to salvation are normally despised, but a more personal invitation given at the right place and the right time is normally more accepted. This lets us to know that when we preach the gospel, we must make relational contacts with the people in question in order to win them to the Lord. When the gospel is preached with indifference or holding people at an arm's length, you cannot properly win souls to the Lord because the spirit of indifference will chase many people away from a loveless call to repentance.

When we lead our preaching with agape love and not with indifference, we will succeed in winning people into the Kingdom the right way by drawing them with the love of Christ that sets strong foundations for their entrance into the Kingdom and then their stability in the house of God.

Gospel Convergence

To converge means "to move towards the same point" or "to join". When God sends an evangelism team into the world to preach the gospel, it is necessary for them to establish a public place of convergence when they conduct their public outreach.

This place of convergence serves as the location of the main public platform from which many people will converge upon to hear the gospel of the Kingdom from your mouth.

This could be a public intersection, a park, a mountain, a beach, city hall, a lake, etc. The important thing is that God will prophetically lead the team to a specific place of convergence that will, in turn, strategically draw large crowds from every direction to come and gather to hear the gospel. Then after this place has been identified and secured for ministry on that given day and time, the team begins preaching the gospel and demonstrating the Kingdom of God with the accompanying signs, wonders, miracles, healing and deliverance to produce a Kingdom harvest.

The drawing grace on the evangelism team will begin to draw large crowds of people from every direction. They will come from neighborhood towns, districts and even other counties to converge upon the public place of meeting in order to get salvation, healing and deliverance.

Please remember that in gospel convergence, the Holy Ghost will always lead the evangelism team to public places of meeting which will yield the greatest strategic impact for that particular section of the town or city.

Gospel convergence is all about saving, healing and delivering souls, but it is also about destroying the influence and government of Satan in that particular town. We see this example of gospel convergence in two separate instance of Luke chapter five.

Luke 5:1 And it came to pass, that, as the people pressed upon him to hear the word of God, he stood by the lake of Gennesaret,

Luke 5:2 And saw two ships standing by the lake: but the fishermen had left out of them, and were washing their nets.

Luke 5:3 And he entered into one of the ships, which was Simon's, **and asked him to thrust out a little from the land. And he sat down, and taught the people out of the ship**.

The lake of Gennesaret was the place of convergence for Jesus to begin to teach the people. In His foreknowledge, Jesus knew how many people would be coming to hear Him teach the Kingdom of God and that is why He strategically had Simon pilot the ship a very small distance from the land in the water so that he could have a strategic vantage point of the entire multitude while the crowd was still in close enough proximity to hear His voice as He taught.

Jesus had just located an unorthodox, but very strategic place of gospel convergence.

Luke 5:15 Yet the news about him spread all the more: **and great multitudes came together to hear, and to be healed by him of their infirmities**.

When we are led by the Holy Spirit to prophetically locate our public place of convergence, this place of prosperity will offer great places of ministry to not only get souls saved, but also heal the sick, perform deliverance ministry, raise the dead and cast out demons. If you ever want to maximize your public platform of evangelism to start breaking the powers of darkness in a region, then find your place of gospel convergence!

Prophetic Pathways

Psalm 119:105 Your word is a lamp for my feet, and a light on my pathway.

Whenever we begin to transact evangelism, we have to not only have a good understanding of the written word of God (logos), but we must also be sensitive to the inspired word of God (rhema). When we have a sensitivity and receptivity to the rhema word, then we will have the necessary prophetic wisdom on when and where to walk our course to reach lost souls that are in need of salvation.

Walking prophetic pathways fulfills the divine, perfect will of God and also secures your evangelistic harvest. Prophetic pathways will always align your course with God's will.

Acts 8:26 And the angel of the Lord spoke to Philip, saying, **<u>Arise, and go toward the south to the way that goes down from Jerusalem to Gaza, which is desert.</u>**

The Lord spoke to Philip to tell him when to get up and where to go. He told Philip to go in a specific direction at a specific time to arrive at a specific location to reap a specific harvest. Remember that prophetic pathways are time-sensitive. When the Lord speaks to you to say "Arise", it means that the time is now! The road you need to walk may have already been built many years beforehand, but God reserves a specific time for you to walk it.

God already knows at what time the person needing evangelism will be at that location and He also knows what time their hearts and minds will be open to the message that you carry.

Open hearts and minds are also time-sensitive.

People may be passionate to get saved at one moment, but if the evangelist misses their time-sensitive prophetic window of opportunity to find and evangelize them, then soon after the window will close.

And once the window has closed, two things can happen. One, the person in question needing salvation may also close their hearts and minds and once again become apathetic and indifferent to the call of repentance to salvation.

What could also happen is that because of the evangelist's disobedience to God to walk their specific prophetic pathway, God may prompt some other evangelist who is willing to be obedient to find that very same person who is seeking Christ and then win them to the Lord. If this happens, the second evangelist will get the soul-winner's reward that was originally supposed to go to the first evangelist simply because they obeyed the will of God in the perfect timing of God. If a space shuttle doesn't hit their specific re-entry window in its designated timeframe as mandated by Flight Control and instead uses its own wisdom to choose another timeframe to re-enter earth's atmosphere, then the shuttle will hit great turbulence upon re-entry and then horribly crash and burn to the ground. Therefore, we must locate and walk our prophetic pathways as soon as the Lord commands us to arise!

Acts 8:27 And he arose and went: and, behold, a man of Ethiopia, a eunuch of great authority under Candace queen of the Ethiopians, who had the charge of all her treasure, and had come to Jerusalem to worship.

Acts 8:28 Was returning and sitting in his chariot, he read Isaiah the prophet.

If Philip did not walk his prophetic pathway as soon as the Lord told him, then he would have missed his evangelism! He would have missed the chariot returning to Egypt from Jerusalem and would have missed out on his mandate and the reward of winning a soul to Christ.

Acts 8:29 Then the Spirit said to Philip, **Go near, and join yourself with this chariot**.

Acts 8:30 And Philip ran towards that place to him, <u>and heard him read the prophet Isaiah</u>, and said, Do you understand what you are reading?

Wisdom allowed Philip to make strategic contact with the Ethiopian eunuch right when the eunuch had become confused and needed clarity and understanding concerning what he was reading. So then Philip began to meet the eunuch right where he was and then bring him from that current level of ignorance to a greater illumination, revelation and understanding of Christ from the Word of God.

Acts 8:31 And he said, **How can I, except some man should guide me? And he desired Philip that he would come up and sit with him**.

Here we see that by Philip following the prophetic instructions of the Lord, a door of access was opened to him to begin to preach Jesus to a man that had an open mind and an open heart. Philip had hit his time-sensitive prophetic pathway and maximized his window of opportunity perfectly!

Acts 8:34 And the eunuch answered Philip and said, I ask you, of whom does this prophet speak? Does he speak of himself, or of some other man?

Acts 8:35 <u>Then Philip opened his mouth and began at the same scripture, and preached Jesus to him</u>.

Here Philip begins to cast the net by preaching the gospel of the Kingdom to the Ethiopian eunuch right from the place of scripture that the eunuch was reading from.

In order to be a wise, skilled and seasoned net caster, you have to be able to preach Jesus Christ from any place of scripture in the bible.

Acts 8:36 And as they went on their way, they came to a certain water: and the eunuch said, **<u>See, here is water; what hinders me to be baptized?</u>**

No doubt that during his preaching discourse to the eunuch, Philip must have talked about the necessity of water baptism.

Acts 8:37 And Philip said, **<u>If you believe with all your heart, then you may.</u>** And he answered and said, **<u>I believe that Jesus Christ is the Son of God</u>**.

Philip understood the principle of belief coupled with repentance. When a person believes with all of their heart, then they will repent. So then by understanding the foundations of a steadfast and total belief of the heart, we should also understand that a person should not get water baptized unless they first fully believe in the Lord Jesus Christ with all their heart. They should not be double-minded or view water baptism as just something new to experiment to pass the time. They must desire water baptism as the next actions subsequent to believing in Jesus Christ. Once belief coupled with repentance has been properly discerned, then that will release the evangelist and the evangelism team to water-baptize the candidate in question. What is awesome and amazing about these two verses of scripture above is that when Philip moved as soon as the Lord told him, he was able to have just enough time to witness to the eunuch about Jesus Christ, the Kingdom of God and what was necessary to enter into the Kingdom of God to produce belief in the eunuch's heart just as the chariot arrived at the baptismal pool. Now that's perfect timing that can only be achieved by walking a prophetic pathway!

Acts 8:38 And he commanded the chariot to stand still: **and they went down both into the water, both Philip and the eunuch; and he baptized him**.

Acts 8:39 And when they were come up out of the water, **the Spirit of the Lord caught Philip away**, and the eunuch saw him no more: **and he went on his way rejoicing**.

Acts 8:40 But Philip was found at Azotus: and passing through he preached in all the cities, till he came to Caesarea.

The fruit of successful evangelism should always produce joy and a spirit of rejoicing within the people that just got saved. The eunuch rejoiced after his salvation as Philip was whisked away by the Holy Spirit to his next assignment. When you begin moving in prophetic evangelism, your ministry will enter into a strong place of acceleration where you will begin to maximize the time that you have by witnessing to the right souls at the right time with strong Kingdom results. Furthermore, when you move prophetically, you will spend the right amount of time witnessing to and winning one group of souls before leaving them to witness to a new group at a strategic time and location using a specific strategy. Remember that the Word of God says that he that wins souls is wise and that is why we must conduct evangelism in prophetic wisdom if we are ever going to see the right harvest. Nothing else can maximize your time and your success in evangelism like the prophetic!

APOSTOLIC EVANGELISM

The Great Publisher

We have learned about the principles and nature of prophetic evangelism. Now we will see how when prophetic evangelism is followed as a standard evangelistic practice, it will grow and blossom into what is known as *apostolic evangelism*.

Apostolic evangelism is the single greatest and most effective global publishing mechanism of the gospel of the Kingdom. It will not only save souls into the Kingdom of God all across the earth, but it will also penetrate, convert and transform human, business and governmental cultures of society throughout the world into strong Kingdom

orientations so that these creatures can transact global dominion through global evangelism.

Psalm 68:11 The Lord gave the word: <u>great was the company of those that published it</u>.

When we examine "word" in this verse, the Hebrew word is "omer" which means a promise or speech. So the context of this verse doesn't pertain solely to the logos word of God (written word), but it also pertains to the rhema word of God directed at His servants concerning precious promises that God has purposed and spoken out of His mouth (inspired word). Remember that He knows the thoughts that He thinks towards us, thoughts of peace and not of evil, to give us an expected end.

The Hebrew word for "publish" is "basar" which means "to announce the good news", "to show forth" and to "tell good tidings".

A "company" is a mass of persons, which points to a large group of people or an army. When we talk about apostolic evangelism, it really brings to life the concept of building a Kingdom army that will globally publish the gospel of the Kingdom.

We already know what evangelism is, but we must first define what "apostolic" means before we can properly understand apostolic evangelism.

To be apostolic means to be sent forth by God.
The Greek word for this is "apostellos". Many people that God sends to preach may go forth in an apostolic

dimension even though they may not have the rank, the authority or the office of an apostle.

There is a difference between being a person that walks in the office of an apostle and being a person that walks in the apostolic dimension. An apostle is one who walks in the apostolic office in a permanent capacity. This means that they carry the rank, authority and grace of one who is sent forth by God to do the work of an apostle in order to reap the harvest of apostolic ministry. When a prophet is sent forth by God on a specific journey or assignment in an apostolic dimension, they then become an "apostolic prophet" for the duration of their assignment. It means that they are still a prophet, but they have just received an upgrade of the apostolic dimension to go forth in a stronger mantle of authority to deal with increased demonic resistance that requires an apostolic dimensional upgrade necessary to topple it.

Please know that the apostolic dimension is only specific for those assignments that God sends them on and does not mean that those servants walk permanently in the office or the mantle of an apostle.

The same principle applies to apostolic evangelism. An evangelist or evangelism team may be sent forth to preach the gospel. When they get an apostolic upgrade, it means that they still walk in the office of the evangelist, but they are now going forth to transact ministry in an apostolic dimension to break down every wall of demonic resistance. This is needed in order to plow rough soils in dry places so that they can sow the word of the gospel into people's hearts. But not only that, when an evangelism team goes forth in apostolic evangelism, they will also have accompanying signs, wonders and miracles to aid them in their demonstration of the Kingdom. This is necessary for the execution of their assignment as they will have to contend with various demonic principalities in cities, territories, regions and nations. They will also have the ability to break the powers of darkness off of a person or people group so that those people can properly hear and obey the gospel and also have the freedom to enter into Kingdom culture.

Now let's look at the traits and hallmarks of apostolic evangelism.

Apostolic evangelism sows the seed of the gospel in wide angles. It is concerned with sowing the seed citywide, regionally, nationally and globally.

Cities Set Upon Hills

Matthew 5:14 Ye are the light of the world. A city that is set on a hill CANNOT be hid.

Apostolic evangelism is focused on taking dominion in the city that God has assigned for it to prosper.

When this happens, church government in a city will join with secular city government to advance the gospel of the Kingdom everywhere within its city limits (which is its territorial sphere). City limits can also serve as the borders of the evangelism team's territorial assignment when dealing with one particular city. This means that the senior leaders of local churches and ministries in the city will join together with saved city councilmen, mayors, judges, local lawmakers, law enforcers and senators to spread the gospel across all of the neighborhoods, districts and counties within that particular city.

This will spread righteousness all throughout the city limits and territorial borders. And that will effectively set cities upon hills because Satan's rule over the city has been cast down and God's rule has been formally established. So then there will first be a spiritual elevation which will place the city in God's favor and then there will be a natural elevation as God will make the city a brilliant spectacle that can be seen by the entire world. When a city is set upon a hill, like Joseph, it will become a strong natural distribution center (abundant natural resources, monetary wealth and a thriving economy) as well as a strong spiritual distribution center (healing, deliverance, spiritual impartation and empowerment) to the entire nation and the world. This is the essence of the Melchisedec priesthood because the city will act in the capacity of a Joseph ministry! It will not only produce solutions to meet people's spiritual needs, but it will also provide solutions that will meet their *natural* needs. We may have the faith to believe that a person can have a ministry of deliverance or that a church can be a house of deliverance, but do we have the faith to believe that our town can be a *city* of deliverance?

When we drive our car to enter into the city limits, will there be an immediate change in the spiritual climate, atmosphere and environment? I believe that God can raise up cities that are set upon hills where people will gain healing and deliverance just as soon as they enter into the city limits! I believe that God can raise up cities that will transform a person's worship and upgrade their prayer life just as soon as they walk into a city or drive their car down the streets of the city. I also believe that God can raise up cities that will manifest signs, wonders and miracles *as the everyday norm* in city life. Do we have the kind of faith to believe that Kingdom culture can become the norm in our cities?

When a city gets saved, then it is the breaking of demonic soul-ties and longstanding generational covenants (and its corresponding curses) with Satan that were created somewhere in that city's past history. This means that the Holy Ghost now has free course in a city to save, deliver, heal, transform, etc. There will be a literal open heaven over the entire city as God's presence, peace, government and glory will rest, rule and abide in that city unhindered and unrestricted. God now has full license and invitation from the city's inhabitants for Him to do a complete work in them and show them off for His glory to the rest of the world because the city has fully and completely submitted to the Lordship of Jesus Christ.

When you see the fulfillment of apostolic evangelism's complete work to manifest the light and glory of Christ over entire territories, you will then begin to see within those territories cities that are set upon hills whose glory shall be beheld by peoples, nations and the entire world.

With apostolic evangelism, you are taking dominion in earnest on a much larger scale than prophetic evangelism ever could. Prophetic evangelism helps you to gain traction in your evangelism and then starts the ball rolling on the *foundations* of dominion. Apostolic evangelism, through Kingdom momentum, progresses your evangelism to the point of *securing* your dominion.

The apostolic dimension upon evangelism allows evangelism to enlarge its net, its territory and its sphere of influence over a larger and wider area of dominion.

Apostolic evangelism will bring the *answered* prayer of Jabez (1 Chronicles 4:10) into modern day manifestation. This means that the entire collection of church ministries within a neighborhood, city or region will band together to form a huge apostolic network. This means that a corporate and cooperative evangelistic effort will effectively cast a giant apostolic net over the entire city to haul in citywide catches! As each neighborhood, district, county, city and region are evangelized, the net will continually widen and enlarge itself as the Kingdom of God advances throughout a region. As wave after wave of demonic opposition is crushed, light begins to spring forth out of an entire region because the net that has been cast begins to increase its line and sphere throughout the earth.

The first levels of apostolic evangelism begin with citywide mobilization.

This is dealing with mobilizing all the saved souls across the entire city to band together in a cohesive and coordinated effort to win the entire city to the Lord. This is not dealing with just saving souls, but it also deals with transforming the man-made systems of that city's society to promote the righteousness of God throughout the city limits. This means that the gospel will have influence in city government.

It will also mold and shape human culture in a territory so that men and women can properly equip themselves with the mind of Christ to execute His divine, perfect will.

When citywide mobilization occurs, then the entire city will begin to elevate in the spirit to fulfill the Matthew 5:14 scripture of being a city that is set upon a hill (as the NET-WORKING book cover illustrates).

This city will then transact dominion everywhere within its borders. The city will reflect the glory and majesty of God in the same fashion that a well-fortified medieval kingdom that God has bestowed great blessing, peace, joy and righteousness upon might display across its entire realm. This is a powerful method of evangelism because you are taking the principles and the harvest of prophetic evangelism and then multiplying that harvest over citywide, region-wide, nationwide and worldwide areas of dominion. This means that more numbers of people are getting saved over a larger area. When global evangelism is achieved, then the scripture that says "For the whole earth shall be full of the knowledge of the glory of the Lord" shall come to pass in great glory!

The Momentum of Apostolic Evangelism

The word "momentum" means a "force or speed of movement". As we look at the momentum of apostolic evangelism, we must first understand that there has to be a catalyst for this momentum.

Furthermore we must also understand that when this momentum is generated, it will then begin to travel in specific directions.

Let's look at how the gospel spreads outward and onward at the time of the 1st century church.

Acts 1:8 But you shall receive power, after the Holy Ghost has come upon you: **and you shall be my witnesses in Jerusalem, and in all Judea, and in Samaria, and to the uttermost part of the earth**.

Jesus Christ is speaking with 11 of the original foundational apostles about how their mandate of dominion would prophetically start from one specific point of origin. Next, he sets the prophetic pathway of the momentum and evangelistic progression of the Church so that she can expand into larger territories over time to then culminate in her global dominion over all of the earth. Remember that the strategy and the prophetic pathway for witnessing the gospel would first begin in Jerusalem, then it would spread to Judea, then to Samaria and then to the rest of the entire earth. Jesus Christ has purposed that the Body of Christ's *enduring* mandate is to take global dominion in the earth.

So here we understand that the catalyst for the momentum of apostolic evangelism began in Jerusalem on the day of Pentecost (Acts Chapter 2). After 3,000 souls were added to the Body of Christ, the Church first began to gain evangelistic traction in Jerusalem and then afterwards she gained apostolic momentum in her evangelism.

We must understand that Jerusalem was situated in the land of Judah. Judah means praise, but it is also the place where the *government of God* went forth. Hebron was the place that David was ordained, but Jerusalem was the place that the city of David was established. So then we understand that Hebron is the place of ordination, but Jerusalem is the place of establishment. Psalm 60:7 says that Judah is the lawgiver and Genesis 49:10 says that the scepter shall not depart from Judah. Here we understand that Jerusalem was the strategic place of ruler-ship and legislation where kings dwelled and transacted governmental business for the entire land.

So then the principle is that when the gospel of the Kingdom is preached and promoted from strategic places of government (whether centralized or decentralized), its harvest will begin to spread all across the land because the gospel is being rendered to the masses from the place of legislation.

This is why Jesus specifically told the original twelve foundational apostles (minus Judas Iscariot) that they must begin witnessing of Him *first* at Jerusalem. Because it is here that the government of Israel would first hear of the gospel of grace and is also where the council of apostles would first be set up. It is the place where the council would also establish the first places of Church governmental authority in strategic places where the laws of the land were created and then legislated to the people. Both natural *and* spiritual governments were set up and established in Jerusalem because Jerusalem was the place of establishment where the Church would begin ruling and reigning on the throne of David to order and establish the government of God in the earth starting from the *place* of government (Isaiah 9:7).

So then we understand that apostolic evangelism cannot truly gain citywide traction and regional momentum unless its discourse first begins in strategic places of government that influence and set policy for the rest of the city.

Once the government of God is established in the place of government, then the Church can begin generating the *increase* of God's government in the earth realm. For this, there will need to be apostolic centers set up in the heart of the city to accomplish this. Our discourse of the gospel through the vehicle of apostolic evangelism must be prophetically aimed at starting from strategic places of governmental influence that will cause Kingdom impact to go forth in the removal of idol worship and unrighteous legislation that holds people in spiritual captivity and bondage. This must be accomplished or else apostolic evangelism cannot gain the proper legal and governmental traction that is necessary to sustain regional momentum and governmental increase. When properly executed, apostolic evangelism will impact and influence governmental legislation.

So then strategically, our evangelism begins in geographical areas that are small in size, but have the ability to influence larger geographical areas as the gospel expands outward and onward. Consider the course and direction that the gospel spreads.

When the gospel spreads outward, it is a sign of evangelism's expansion. When the gospel spreads onward, it is a sign of evangelism's progression.

So as our evangelism begins to take root in small geographical areas of influence, it will eventually expand its territorial borders and its spheres of influence to occupy larger geographical areas of dominion.

Back during the times of the reign of the kings of Israel after the death of Solomon, the kingdom of Israel was split into the Northern Kingdom (10 tribes of Israel and their regions) and the Southern Kingdom (the tribe and region of Judah). Even after the land had come under Roman occupation, Jesus never forgot the ancient territorial borders of Israel and that is why he said to start first in Jerusalem (the capitol city of Judah).

Once the gospel gained traction and establishment with the city's kings (people of affluence, wealth and authority) in the strategic place of government, it could then expand its scope to include the larger territory of Judea (the entire land of Judah). Once Judea had been evangelized, then that would signify the completion of the gospel's discourse to the entire tribe of Judah, including all of its borders. Then from there, the apostles could now turn their attention to Samaria which is the region and territory of the ten other tribes of Israel. After Samaria was completed, then that would also complete the entire nation of Israel. From there, the Gentile world could now hear the gospel to the uttermost parts of the earth in proper prophetic timing and apostolic order. Notice that it did not say "uttermost parts of the world", it said, "uttermost parts of the earth". Because the word of God says that the gospel of the Kingdom will be preached in not just the entire world system, but to the entire ends of the earth.

1st Century Evangelism

Now that we understand the importance of apostolic evangelism's discourse to governments, let us now look at how the 1st century Church's discourse of evangelism traveled.

Acts 1:13 And when they had come in, they went up into an upper room, where Peter, and James, and John, and Andrew, Philip, and Thomas, Bartholomew, and Matthew, James the son of Alphaeus, and Simon Zelotes, and Judas the brother of James abided.

Acts 1:14 These all continued with one accord in prayer and supplication, with the women, and Mary the mother of Jesus, and his brethren.

After Jesus ascended into heaven, the apostles and the women went into prayer and intercession in the upper room. The women served as intercessors and spiritual midwives that went into prayer and supplication to aid the apostles with prayer and strategic intercessions that were needed to birth out into earthly manifestation a new dispensation of a greater priesthood (Melchisedec) which included: greater worship, greater sacrifices, greater ministries, greater works and greater exploits into the earth realm. This dispensation (time period) is known as the dispensation of grace.

So then the principle is that prayer births out new prophetic movements that are needed to usher in new times and seasons.

As the new times and seasons of grace entered into manifestation, those that were in the upper room got saved and then those people that also heard the preaching of the gospel on the day of Pentecost also got saved. From there on, the gospel began to increase and the number of believers and disciples also began to increase and multiply over the next four chapters of the book of Acts.

Levels of Expansion

When we examine different levels of expansion, we will find that at each level of expansion, our nets will begin to widen. When our nets continually widen at each level of expansion, it will signify that apostolic evangelism is in operation.

The awesome machine of apostolic evangelism by nature is a vehicle of expansion and progression with two main aspects of duality in its dynamic:

1. Outward Expansion

2. Onward Expansion

The two main dynamics of expansion in apostolic evangelism is to expand the gospel of the Kingdom outward and onward.

When it expands outward, it is the dynamic of expanding the gospel outward from a central hub (apostolic center) within a city throughout the territorial borders of that city. When apostolic evangelism expands onward, it is the dynamic of progressing the expansion of the gospel onward to other cities and regions outside of the original hub. This means that apostolic evangelism first expands outward from an apostolic center within the city so that it converts the entire city. From there, it expands onward to plant another hub or apostolic center in other cities and then repeats the same process as before to convert those cities and regions. Onward expansion goes through a progressive-level dynamic which has an adjustable blueprint for multiple city conversions depending on the prophetic strategy released from God on how to take each respective city.

Onward expansion may set up apostolic centers in each city so that each city can properly branch the gospel outward from a central hub and then once the city has been taken, they can also repeat the process of branching onward to different cities and regions as God leads them.

Each city may also have its own separate blueprint because the demonic principalities that reside over one city are not the same principalities that you will encounter in other cities. Sometimes many cities within one specific region may have the same principalities, but you will normally encounter different principalities when you travel to different regions. These new principalities may operate in different functions to release different levels of perversion that the first region did not release. So once you arrive in a different region, you may need to seek God in prayer for different strategies on how to take that respective region.

Within the two main levels of outward and onward expansion, there lies an additional four levels of tiered groups of expansion.

1. Citywide mobilization

2. Regional expansion

3. National expansion

4. Global expansion

There are different and diverse levels of expansion within the apostolic network. When these dynamics come into play, there is first a *spiritual* expansion as the territory in question undergoes spiritual reformation, revival, restoration, empowerment, transformation and then advancement.

People must first experience an *inner* spiritual expansion (spirit man revivals, growth and maturity in grace, mind renewals and life transformations) to expand their individual capacities before they can move into outward and onward levels of expansion to naturally and spiritually expand the capacities of cities, territories and regions.

I must stress this again. Only when these spiritual expansions have been completed, then can the *natural* expansions follow as a direct result of the corporate spiritual breakthrough and deliverance in a territory that's been established in the spirit realm.

The four inner tiered levels of expansion within the apostolic network expand *inwards* to penetrate, convert and transform the cultures of cities within the target scope while the two main levels of expansion will expand *outwards* and *onwards* to lengthen and widen the net so that the gospel spreads across territories and regions.

Kingdom Multiplication

One of the most powerful concepts you will learn that governs the corporate dynamic of expansion in apostolic evangelism is the principles of Kingdom Multiplication.

Acts 6:7 <u>And the word of God increased; and the number of the disciples multiplied in Jerusalem greatly</u>; <u>and a great company of the priests were obedient to the faith</u>.

As we examine the process of citywide mobilization, let's follow the biblical pattern of this in Acts 6:7. Here we see the firm establishment of the gospel in Israel's capitol city of Jerusalem. The word of God increased throughout the city of Jerusalem and the number of disciples multiplied.

A disciple is a learner, a student and a follower of Christ. In order for you to become a disciple, you must undergo a conversion into discipleship. Conversion happens in your mind, your heart and your spirit man.

Once these things are converted and you are being obedient to follow the perfect will of God, then you have now become an effective disciple of Christ.

What is awesome about this level of expansion is that you don't have just a large quantity of saved people, but you also have a large quantity of saved *disciples*. Being a believer does not automatically make you a disciple of Christ, but every disciple of Christ is already a believer. Notice that the scripture did not say that the number of "believers" multiplied. It says that the number of "disciples" multiplied.

This is significant because apostolic evangelism cannot gain traction through the multiplication of believers. Apostolic evangelism can only gain traction and momentum through the multiplication of disciples.

You cannot win cities to the Lord if you don't have disciples. We have many believers all over the globe, but because many of those believers have not made the transition into discipleship, they cannot transform their cities.

A lot of believers don't know the principles of binding and loosing. They don't know the principles of prophetic and apostolic intercession and they don't know how to release the supernatural over their cities. They don't know how to sense spiritual climate shifts or how to set prophetic atmospheres. They don't know how to generate substantial wealth creation or facilitate wealth transfers. They don't know how to take these wealth creations and transfers to then roll them over into business capital that is needed to execute strong business mandates. They don't know how to create resources that will aid them in generating business and ministry expansion so that they can transform governmental systems and structures into Kingdom orientations. But disciples do!

So it is not Kingdom believers, but it is Kingdom discipleship that produces sons of God that will ultimately multiply your local church numbers outward into all of the mountains of culture to make them relevant for modern day application and influential decision-making in today's government and society.

This is what is needed to mobilize an army of disciples that can sound the clarion call to assemble a citywide mobilization that is needed to produce citywide dominion.

Please understand that disciples are still believers, but they are now believers that have gone through several growth processes of maturity after salvation. These growth processes include: suffering for Christ, denying the flesh and ungodliness and effectively eradicating the immaturity of former novices to now garner the perfected maturity of full-grown sons of God. Their gifts and their fruit will have matured. After those processes are complete, they are now armed with preparation, empowerment, strategy, authority and maturity to transact dominion as full-grown sons of the Kingdom.

Because not only do you have a huge quantity of saints, but that same quantity is also a huge number of quality saints, who are believers and disciples rolled into one.

That's the key to expansion and that's the hallmark to cultivating strong barometers of success in apostolic evangelism. This is the principle and the standard that many mega-churches need to implement within their own blueprint so that their boast won't be about the quantity of numbers that they have, but their joy will be found in the number of quality disciples that they have. We should never boast about or draw attention to our congregational numbers if those numbers haven't been properly discipled into sons of God.

Ministry Through Multiplication

So as we continue learning the principles of multiplication, we find that the number of disciples multiplied greatly.

Remember that Kingdom expansion focuses on and is dependent on the principles of multiplication.

When the multiplication of the disciples began to happen in the early church, many other ministries were birthed out of this multiplication.

There was first a multiplication in disciples, but there was also a multiplication of different ministries being birthed within the Body of Christ.

Consider the great things that were birthed by apostolic evangelism:

1. Apostolic ministry

2. Prophetic ministry

3. Prayer ministry

4. Evangelism ministry

5. Healing and Deliverance ministry

6. Discipleship

7. Signs, Wonders and Miracles

8. Cell Ministries

9. The Founding of Local Churches

10. Establishment of Local and Corporate Church Government

11. Establishment of Bishopricks

12. Deacons Ministries (deacons served tables and resolved widows' matters)

13. Wealth Creations and Transfers

These thirteen dimensions of Church ministry were all harvested from the initial seed of apostolic evangelism that was planted into good ground in the governmental place of divine establishment (Jerusalem). What's awesome about this is that this level of Kingdom production was harvested in only the first five chapters subsequent to the institution of the Church (Acts chapter 2). This means that multiple aspects of Kingdom ministry could be birthed and multiplied quickly. But not just multiplied in one direction. It could be multiplied in many directions! Remember that the principles of Kingdom multiplication follow the same patterns of Kingdom expansion. There is multiplication outward and then there is multiplication onward. The Kingdom starts out as a very small mustard seed, but then over time it establishes its roots downward to gain a strong foundation and stability so that it can grow upward into a great tree that has the ability to produce increase and on-going harvest where birds can lodge on its branches.

Multiplication deals with growth because disciples grow in grace and in number. So then in its infancy before its public discourse, the preparatory prayers needed to usher in the Church Age was first prepared for in the upper room with eleven foundational apostles, women, the earthly family of Jesus Christ (Mary and His brethren) and then established in Jerusalem on the Day of Pentecost with the twelve apostles (Matthias was added to their apostolic ranks). As 3,000 souls began to be added to the Kingdom, the Church began to expand its reach by branching outward and onward to other cities and regions of the nation of Israel.

Hallmarks of Citywide Mobilization

Apostolic evangelism, by nature, is a very strong locomotive, even at its initial inception and institution before it has even accomplished anything. The key, however, to this locomotive flourishing and excelling is *to get it up to speed.*

Acts 6:7 marks the first level of expansion and acceleration within apostolic evangelism:

Citywide mobilization

When the entire city mobilizes, it is the entire church of God that is located in that particular city that mobilizes together to cast a huge net over the entire city. This means that the entire city is converted to salvation, deliverance and empowerment. Prayer cultures will begin to govern and legislate the heavens above the city to yield a prophetic harvest for citywide direction in order to dictate the course and pathway of dominion. Prophecy will be the norm. Visions, dreams, signs, wonders and miracles will increase and also be the norm. Worship will begin to release great impartation over the land to cause healing to come to not only people, but nature, forests and the entire plant kingdom within its territorial borders. Nature will begin to sing!

As worship moves over the waters and seas, the waves will begin to respond to heavenly worship with unique and specific ripple patterns to indicate its response to the Kingdom's universal call to worship. Corporate worship will become completely unified across the entire city as every church and every system begins to come into perfect agreement to establish powerful worship and prayer altars throughout the city so that the city can come together to glorify God with one mouth and one voice.

As the city is spiritually converted, you will begin to see human culture, business culture and governmental culture come into alignment and harmony so that the "creatures" of the city come to a place of repentance, revolutionary change and transformation to give God the glory.

You will see natural conversions appear into manifestation as the spiritual climates and atmospheres begin to change and literally transform city cultures so that the Kingdom of God is the dominant culture that will be the visible norm throughout the entire city. Racial, cultural and socio-economic barriers will be cast down and agape love will abound as the city comes together in the unity of the Holy Spirit.

You will truly see a city set upon a hill that will shine as a brilliant spectacle to other lands and regions!

Regional Expansion

Acts 8:1 And Saul was consenting to his death. And at that time there was a great persecution against the church which was at Jerusalem; **and they were all scattered abroad throughout the regions of Judea and Samaria**, except the apostles.

Acts 8:4 Therefore they that were scattered abroad went everywhere preaching the word.

Acts 8:5 Then Philip went down to the city of Samaria, and preached Christ to them.

Remember that at each stage of expansion and acceleration, the machine will continually pick up the pace and quicken the momentum of apostolic evangelism so that the machine will start traveling at a faster pace. The pace of apostolic evangelism is similar to the pace of a train locomotive. It lumbers out of the train station at a very slow pace and then over the next few minutes it begins gathering traction, velocity and momentum to then travel at a high rate of speed in order to reach its destinations in a shorter amount of time. Once it reaches a high rate of speed, the train is virtually unstoppable. Outside forces will not be able to stop the train once it has gathered and sustained this kind of momentum and only the train conductor (Jesus Christ) can stop the locomotive. So the way that God makes the train go to faster speeds is to allow great opposition and persecution to give the train a strong push from behind so that the train can get up to speed and travel at a faster rate.

So then the principle is that once apostolic evangelism has gained a high rate of speed and is able to sustain its velocity by demonic opposition and persecution, the world and the devil cannot stop its momentum!

For this reason, Acts 8:1-5 marks the 2nd level of expansion and acceleration in apostolic evangelism. This level of expansion is known as:

Regional Expansion

This new level was given to the Church at the proper prophetic timing after the 1st level of expansion had already been mastered. Here we see God allowing persecution to hit the church at Jerusalem to scatter the word of God quickly and the seed of the Kingdom (disciples of Christ) began to spread outward and onward at a faster rate than the 1st level could so that the gospel could now have access to Israel's other regions of Judea and Samaria in a shorter amount of time. But this level of access could not be penetrated until the twelve foundational apostles first yielded to the prophetic placement of God to establish the Church first at Jerusalem.

Once the Church was established there, God began to give them access to expand the gospel into other regions using the principles of discipleship and multiplication. Here we see a prophetic shift in focus and a strong apostolic push into larger and wider territorial areas in order to evangelize the rest of the regions of Judea (southern kingdom) and Samaria (northern kingdom). Remember that God recognizes the ancient landmarks (territorial boundaries) and borders of ancient Israel as He intended and that is why he strategically tells the Church to possess all of the lands that are throughout the totality of their territory as He declares it and how He envisions it.

Remember that the first level of expansion within apostolic evangelism is first aimed at converting a city. The second level of expansion is aimed at converting regions.

When you go through different levels of expansion, do remember that there will be demonic opposition to your net-working because the devil does not want his prisoners to go free. Remember that persecution and suffering for Christ is always working for your good even though you may not realize it at the time.

God used the vehicle of persecution to begin to scatter the seed of the Kingdom so that they could evangelize two regions of Israel (Judea and Samaria) *simultaneously*. After going through strong discipleship and multiplication, the Church was in a much stronger position to enlarge her territories in several different directions in quicker amounts of time.

As Philip entered into the city of Samaria and began to preach the gospel, it began to break the powers of darkness in that region so that the people of Samaria were no longer under its sway and influence.

The preaching of the gospel, along with the agency of the anointing, signs, wonders and miracles, began to penetrate people's uncircumcised ears and hearts to produce strong levels of faith in the word of God and then that is when the people gave heed to the gospel. Not only that, but the preaching of the gospel began to produce Kingdom atmospheres that were conducive to casting out unclean spirits, healing people with palsies and causing lame men to walk.

As a result of this type of deliverance, there was great joy in the entire city. **Remember that joy is a strong hallmark and harvest of successful evangelistic ministry.** And this is because strong evangelistic ministry broke the powers of witchcraft off of the people so that they could hear and obey the gospel to have peace and joy. Delivering the city from the power of Satan opened up more doors of evangelistic opportunity for Philip to preach the gospel to other Samaritan villages in the region. So we have to notice the transitions between the different levels of expansion and then recognize the hallmarks of whether it is a citywide mobilization or a regional expansion.

The 2nd level of regional expansion in apostolic evangelism builds upon the 1st level of citywide mobilization to achieve greater levels of multiplication.

The 1st level is only aimed at multiplication within a single city whereas the 2nd level is aimed at multiplication within several regions. But here on the 2nd level, the *answered* prayer of Jabez (to enlarge his coasts) is coming into manifestation and operation through a greater dynamic and greater speed to enlarge the borders of your evangelism and the coasts of your influence.

National Expansion

We now arrive at the 3rd level of expansion in apostolic evangelism:

National Expansion

Using the same principles of discipleship and multiplication, our evangelistic multiplier begins to go into upper echelons of multiplication and national levels of expansion.

When apostolic evangelism has a national mandate, an entire country and nation will first gain salvation and then undergo Kingdom conversions and transformations.

These countries' orientation, business processes and governmental laws will truly model the Kingdom of God, reflect the righteousness of God and give glory to His name in word and deed.

Using the United States for example, this country is split up into four main regions: The West, the Midwest, the Northeast and the South. Among these four regions, the West is comprised of the 13 states that are located in the western region of the United States. These states include Alaska, Hawaii, California, Oregon, Nevada, Washington State, Arizona, Utah, Idaho, Wyoming, Montana, Colorado and New Mexico.

These states would have been converted by apostolic evangelism at the 2nd level of regional expansion. Now imagine the gargantuan jump in multiplication we will have when we join our apostolic nets at prophetically strategic bridging points within this country that will widen the nets to be large enough to fit the harvest of all 50 states within its volume. Can you imagine this entire nation being caught in one giant apostolic net? Remember that each level of expansion releases a greater glory than the previous level before it. So when all four regions of the country are properly connected and bridged, then the glory that will be released from that connection will be unparalleled in United States history!

The executive branch of federal government including the presidents of the United States will give God the glory in all of their thinking, their decision making and the laws that they enforce. The legislative branch will gain deliverance from ungodly anti-Christ influences and then armed with the mind of Christ, they will begin to create and enact into legislation laws that reflect the righteousness of God to ultimately give God glory.

They will no longer make policies that legalize wickedness, perversion and other unrighteous acts and deeds that commit high treason against the sovereignty of God.

The judicial branch including the Supreme Court, state courts, federal courts, municipal courts, appellate courts and all of their presiding judges that sit on their respective benches, will no longer interpret city, state and federal laws with the intention of keeping conformity with the spirit of the world, but they will now interpret these laws by the wisdom of God. Then the jury will render their verdicts according to the mind of Christ.

All three branches of government within the United States will begin to operate in prophetic synergy and syncopation to transform the kingdoms of this country into the kingdoms of our Lord and of His Christ. How glorious!

Global Expansion

Here is our 4th and final level of expansion: Global Expansion. This is the act of taking our apostolic evangelism worldwide and then using our apostolic networks on each continent of the earth to bridge and cover the entire globe. The level of multiplication at this stage is off the charts as billions of disciples are created, multiplied and then dispersed to move across the face of the entire earth to convert all nations and continents with the gospel of the Kingdom.

The nations of the earth will show forth the glory of God in its entire splendor. Ambassadors from several countries and nations will be converted and then be on one mind and one accord with Kingdom agendas and mindsets when they sit down to have talks in the United Nations. They will no longer argue, bicker or squabble about world foreign policy, but kings will come together to pray to the throne of God in order to get the mind of Christ. Then they will come into spiritual agreement with each other once they receive the answer from heaven.

They will come together to share revelation, wisdom and knowledge in order to develop apostolic and prophetic blueprints for not only their nations, but for the entire globe. And then when God speaks prophetically in their midst at their UN (United Nations) summits, they will move quickly into agreement and then begin to apostolically set universal policy for the entire globe based off of the mind of Christ and the patterns of heaven. There won't be a need for NATO (North American Treaty Organization) anymore since nations will not be studying to go to war with each other.

When global expansion occurs, you will see the will of heaven literally manifest in the entire earth in full measure. The whole earth will embrace the knowledge and the glory of God and then govern its entire operations strongly by the culture of heaven. The earth will be in agreement with heaven so that God will have eternal access, relationship and habitation to eternally tabernacle with His creation and His people unhindered.

Then shall this scripture come to pass:

Habbakuk 2:14 <u>For the earth shall be filled with the knowledge of the glory of the LORD, as the waters cover the sea</u>.

God has purposed this to happen through the powerful machine of apostolic evangelism!

<u>The Model of Apostolic Evangelism</u>

Let's look at the model of Apostolic Evangelism which includes the catalyst, the progression and the fulfillment of it from seed stage to harvest.

1. Individuals get saved

Here is where individual persons come to the place of repentance which will then lead to them partaking of the New Birth born-again experience, followed by transformation through discipleship to attain son-ship.

2. Families get saved to form local churches

Family salvations are the next level of progression. Saved families are very important to building the momentum of apostolic evangelism. If families cannot get saved, then it will halt the momentum of apostolic evangelism and then raise questions concerning credibility later on at the formation of a local church when the head of the house becomes an overseer of a household that may or may not include his own unsaved family. This will tarnish his credibility and sabotage the progression of the local church.

Remember that the heads of households' first work of corporate ministry is to minister the gospel of the Kingdom to their own families.

1 Timothy 3:1 This is a true saying, If a man desires the office of a bishop, he desires a good work.

1 Timothy 3:4 <u>One that rules well his own house, having his children in subjection with all honor</u>;

1 Timothy 3:5 <u>For if a man knows not how to rule his own house, how shall he take care of the church of God?</u>

Here is where the questions of a man of God's credibility and spiritual fitness for the office of a bishop or overseer is examined and deemed fit or unfit for public office and service. If he and his family are saved and are walking in the Spirit, then they will all be in spiritual agreement and the house will be in godly order that will then make him credible and eligible to execute the office of an overseer at God's call and ordination.

Let's look at some local churches that were located in family homes in scripture.

Colossians 4:15 Salute the brethren which are in Laodicea, and Nymphas, **<u>and the church which is in his house</u>**.

We must understand that the foundations of forming local churches begin within family homes.

Many local churches started out small with two or three saved families and then grew in number as more families got saved. Nymphas was a Colossian saint of God who lived in the city of Laodicea that was the overseer of a local church in his own house. If Nymphas got saved, but the house of Nymphas never got saved, then the atmosphere of his home would not be conducive for ushering in the presence of God since his home would be out of order. God is not the author of confusion. God's presence cannot reside in a house of spiritual disorder and unrest and His government cannot be established in a house of spiritual dysfunction.

So then the saved head of the home and his unsaved wife and children will ultimately tarnish his corporate witness to other families that come to visit his church services because the preached messages and promises of a better hope and a better life are not being manifested and modeled in his own home. This will ultimately provide a false witness to other people that come into the house looking for salvation because the first family of that local church is not properly modeling the Kingdom of God in their own lives.

The first family of a local church must first provide a strong working model that is clearly visible and tangible so that other families can bear witness to that light and that model to then follow that pattern of Kingdom excellence in their own marriages and family lifestyles.

Dramatic examples of the Kingdom are needed from leadership so that the laity can duplicate these models of excellence in their own homes.

Philemon 1:2 And to our beloved Apphia, and Archippus our fellow soldier, **and to the church in your house**.

Philemon was a man who also led a local church in his own house and that is why the Apostle Paul sent an epistle to be read in Philemon's house which is the same place that his local church was also located.

When families get saved, then their entire household will begin to change the culture of how they think, speak, believe, behave and live.

When the hearts and minds of family members change, then that is when family culture will change. So when the gospel of the Kingdom pierces the hearts and minds of an entire family, then it will also penetrate the culture of the entire family tree to establish a generational legacy of blessings within that particular family bloodline.

Furthermore, the generational curses which previously resided within that particular family bloodline will be broken and its negative traits and effects reversed so that the entire family tree can go forth, prosper and have good success and blessings as they live joyfully for God.

In time, after families have grown in grace, wisdom, knowledge, maturity and the love of our Lord and Savior, they can then form a cell ministry. Cell ministries are small groups that mainly congregate in homes. These cell ministries can then begin to be planted within family homes (assuming the head of the house gets saved and receives the mandate from God to conduct them). These cell ministries can provide in-home prayer gatherings, in-home bible studies, in-home worship services and in-home counseling services that will bless, refresh, revive, strengthen and encourage families as they walk their course of destiny in God.

Let's look at an example of an entire home that receives the gospel.

Acts 16:31 And they said, **Believe on the Lord Jesus Christ, and you and your house shall be saved**.

Acts 16:32 And they spoke the word of the Lord to him **and to all that were in his house**.

Acts 16:33 And he took them the same hour of the night, and washed their stripes; and was baptized, **he and all his**, immediately.

Acts 16:33 And when he had brought them into his house, he set meat before them, and rejoiced, **believing in God with his entire house**.

When evangelism is properly positioned, presented and demonstrated to an entire family in power, authority and grace in the prophetic timing of God, then that entire house will get saved.

Great generational legacies in entire family trees and bloodlines can be formed simply because of one head of the house's faith and obedience to believe the gospel, get saved and live for the Lord. As soon as Paul was finished getting the Philippian jailor's house saved, he then entered into *another* home to conduct more house ministry (Acts 16:40).

While many mega-churches focus on racking up thousands of members to boast about their numbers in order to give themselves the glory and receive the praises of men, true evangelism is focused on winning cities one soul at a time to give God the glory.

The wonderful thing about apostolic evangelism is that even though it amasses large numbers for the purpose of taking the city, it still doesn't adopt secular thinking that treats individuals as just another number that many worldly churches do, but instead focuses on getting entire families saved and not just one individual. Every life is precious and every soul is loved. One can make the difference! Remember that there is joy in heaven over one soul that comes to repentance!

3. Local churches begin to spread the gospel to convert neighborhoods

Once many families get saved within a neighborhood, then those families can group together to form a local church. Once this process is repeated often enough, local church plants can then begin to sprout up in many different neighborhoods. These local churches will be raised up in strategic areas of placement to convert and bridge different neighborhoods together. As neighborhoods are converted, the cell ministries conducted inside homes within neighborhoods will begin to blossom. Homeowners and homeowners associations (HOA) will start to be impacted by the gospel and then begin to legislate neighborhood policy with laws and standards that reflect and represent the righteousness of God. Neighborhood community watches will begin to be strengthened by the unity of the Spirit and the fellowship of the saints. There will be such a peace and a liberty and a safety that you will tangibly feel as you are walking through these neighborhoods.

The leaders of entire HOA boards of different subdivisions within a single neighborhood will begin to come together with one mind and one accord to set corporate neighborhood policy that implements the standards of godly righteousness within our communities. Bear in mind that the HOA governs the policies and procedures of neighborhood subdivisions that contain *hundreds* of homes. Greed and preferential treatment towards the rich and against the poor will be eradicated. With the removal of greed will also come the elimination of the overcharging of homeowners' insurance premiums, property and casualty insurance premiums and other excessive miscellaneous fees and costs that are needed to maintain these homes and neighborhoods. The mandate won't be to control and regulate homeowners in a dogmatic, legalistic way, but instead the love of God that brings compassion will begin to overtake their hearts as they begin to adhere to the principles of righteousness when they go forth to legislate and set neighborhood policy that benefits everyone and not just themselves.

This will then give rise to the planting of strong local churches at strategic points of intersection within a neighborhood that will ultimately bridge neighborhood communities together in a unified worship to God.

When we bridge neighborhoods, it is the process of unifying neighborhoods together in corporate synergy and syncopation with one mind and one accord so that the momentum of apostolic evangelism will continue to spread outward and onward.

These local churches will begin to grow in abundance and also grow into strong relationships with each other to form neighborhood networks. When these nets are properly joined, it will then bridge neighborhoods together to begin to glorify God with one mouth and one voice in the unity of the Spirit.

The key to neighborhood networking lies in our ability to cast our nets down and then join them together *as one*. This will expand our nets so that they will have the ability to bridge entire neighborhoods. As our nets expand, so shall our evangelism also continue to expand. As we combine our nets collectively to bridge different neighborhoods in a cooperative evangelistic effort, our nets will begin to lengthen and widen outward and onward as we begin to harvest more souls and more territory for the Kingdom.

4. Neighborhoods spread the gospel to convert districts

As bridged neighborhoods begin to scatter the seed of the gospel outward in a concentrated effort to convert many districts and its municipalities, this will signify the beginning of evangelistic influence in the *creatures* of city government and the officials who govern these creatures. The gospel will begin to convert business owners who run entrepreneurships, small businesses and large corporations. Districts will also begin to integrate saved disciples into public offices. These offices include elected public officials such as city councilmen and city councilwomen.

Once they are converted, they will begin to influence public policy through natural legislation as well as Kingdom legislation (declarations and decrees). Districts will begin to institute programs run by pastors to provide housing and shelters for transients, orphans, vagabonds, widows and the homeless. Once these shelters are instituted, then pastors will come in to execute deliverance and love ministries to those that are in those shelters in order to mend those broken hearts and heal their wounds of rejection. Here is where apostolic evangelism will begin to gain traction in the government sector which influences city policy.

5. Districts spread the gospel to convert counties

Here the same process of discipleship, multiplication and outward expansion progresses and continues to bridge all districts together in a single county.

6. Counties spread the gospel to convert cities

The disciples in all counties within a city multiply outward and then bridge all counties within a city together to convert the city. Then the disciples multiply and move onward to repeat this process in other cities for multiple city conversions.

7. Cities spread the gospel to convert regions

All cities within a region multiply their disciples outward and onward to bridge cities together within a region. This process is repeated to convert multiple regions.

8. Regions spread the gospel to convert nations

All regions within a nation bridge their regions together at strategic bridging points to convert the entire nation including the capitol city or capitol district of that nation. This process is repeated to convert many nations.

9. Nations spread the gospel across the earth and penetrate every kingdom and culture to convert the entire world.

And finally, the number of disciples will multiply into the billions to expand outward and onward across the entire globe to convert every nation and continent and then bridge them together so that the whole earth is filled with the knowledge of the glory of the Lord.

The system of the world would no longer influence mankind, but it is the Kingdom of God that will govern every element of human, business and governmental cultures. All earthly kingdoms have now undergone and completed all Kingdom conversions and transformations.

The kingdoms of this world have now become the kingdoms of our Lord Jesus and His Christ (the Church). Hallelujah and Amen!

THE CONCLUSION OF THE MATTER

We have come to the end of a long and amazing journey through the wonderful world of NETWORKING! Prayerfully you can take the revelatory principles, wisdom and knowledge contained in this book, apply them to your life and then start moving in transformation and forward progression in your individual salvation to save your own soul and also your evangelism ministry to save other people's souls.

Remember that this book teaches evangelism from a Kingdom perspective and a dominion worldview so that it reveals heavenly revelation, wisdom, knowledge and strategy for your establishment in the present truth concerning 21st century evangelism. As such, this present truth will catapult you into strong levels of Kingdom advancement. It is my prayer that after reading this book, you have become well-versed on the subject of evangelism and its great importance as a vital component and viable blueprint for fulfilling your dominion mandate in the earth.

Get excited about your future in evangelism as God has many exploits lined up for you and many lives that you must touch so start preparing for your harvest! Receive the equipping of this book to become a disciple of Christ. Use the revelatory vehicles of evangelism to take dominion in strategic areas of your life and the territorial sphere that God has graced you to possess. May the Lord bless you and keep you and give you great grace and favor to occupy the earth until He comes!

It's time to embrace your destiny as a dominion chaser!

www.ingramcontent.com/pod-product-compliance
Lightning Source LLC
Chambersburg PA
CBHW070645160426
43194CB00009B/1580